BREAD OF TOMORROW

D11189880

BREAD OF TOMORROW

Prayers for the Church Year

Janet Morley, editor

ORBIS BOOKS

Maryknoll, New York 10545

The Catholic Foreign Mission Society of America (Maryknoll) recruits and trains people for overseas missionary service. Through Orbis Books, Maryknoll aims to foster the international dialogue that is essential to mission. The books published, however, reflect the opinions of their authors and are not meant to represent the official position of the society.

Compilation and editorial matter © Christian Aid 1992
Copyright on individual items remains with the authors

All rights reserved
Published by Orbis Books, Maryknoll, NY 10545

First published in Great Britain in 1992 by SPCK, Holy Trinity Church, Marylebone Road, London NW1 4DU and Christian Aid, P.O. Box 100, London SE1 7RT

Christian Aid, an official agency of 41 British and Irish churches, is committed to strengthening the poor in more than 70 countries worldwide.

Manufactured in the United States of America

Library of Congress Cataloging-in-Publication Data

Bread of tomorrow : prayers for the church year / Janet Morley, editor.
    p. cm.
  ISBN 0-88344-831-9 (pbk.)
  1. Prayers. 2. Church year—Prayer-books and devotions—English.
  I. Morley, Janet.
  BV245.B6395 1992
  242'.8—dc20

                                     92-5619
                                       CIP

ACKNOWLEDGMENTS

We are grateful to all the authors and publishers who have given permission for their material to appear in this book, and apologize to any copyright holder whom we have been unable to trace.

The following texts are taken from WCC Publications, World Council of Churches, Geneva, Switzerland:

"When I'm down and helpless" (p. 14) and "O God: Enlarge my heart" (p. 24), *With All God's People: The New Ecumenical Prayer Cycle,* 1989.

"Today I look into my own heart" (p. 21) and "When the day comes" (p. 118), *Why O Lord? Psalms and Sermons from Namibia,* 1987.

"If we have worshiped you" (p. 17), *Worship Resources,* World Conference on Mission and Evangelism, 1989.

"I believe that behind the mist" (p. 113), *Confessing Our Faith Around the World IV, South America,* 1985.

"Brothers and sisters in creation" (p. 151) is taken from "The Rainbow Covenant" devised by the International Consultancy on Religion, Education and Culture (ICOREC) and the World Wide Fund for Nature (WWF), and first used in the Winchester Creation Harvest Liturgy (England), 1987.

Special thanks are due to those who helped to select the material: Lesley Anderson, Jan Berry, Marigold Best, Kate Compston, Kathy Galloway, Maggie Hamilton, Robert Pearce, Jeffrey Williams.

Orbis Books thanks Janet Morley, Christian Aid, and SPCK, who graciously permitted modifications for this edition.

CONTENTS

Index of Prayer Types   169

INTRODUCTION

Abba, our God,
whom the heavens disclose,
may your name be held holy,
your authority come.
May your longing be fulfilled
as in heaven, so on earth.
Give us today
the bread of tomorrow,
and cancel our debts
as we have already
forgiven our debtors.
Do not draw us in
to sinful enticement
but set us free
from the grip of evil;
for authority and power and glory
are yours alone, for ever.
Amen.

Alternative Service Book, 1980

There is a great deal of interest in churches today about how Christians are formed and how faith is learned and developed and shared in the modern world. The practice of prayer is central, because this is where we offer ourselves to be shaped by the gospel we long to share. And public prayer gathers us together to be shaped as communities that seek to live out that gospel. But what is prayer, and what kind of gospel do our prayers witness to?

For What Do We Pray?

Even the most familiar and basic prayer of Christians, the Lord's Prayer, may be prayed and understood in very different ways, as the translation above from Matthew's Gospel suggests. Are we asking, with Luke, for the reassurance of "daily bread" — strength to keep going in a world that we expect to continue much as it is now? Or are we, with Matthew, pressing urgently to be given today "the bread of tomorrow" — the Messianic feast for the poor that is a sign of a totally different world order?

On the whole, I have chosen the first approach. Most of us find the Lord's Prayer familiar and comforting, not unsettling or full of painful longing. Not actually hungry for bread, most of us pray for spiritual stamina day by day. We pray for forgiveness of our personal sins, and we celebrate a spiritual kingdom of power and glory that somehow authorizes and blesses the systems in which we presently live.

Many Christians in the poorest parts of our world pray quite differently. They pray for real food, but they are also hungry for justice; they long for freedom from the intolerable burdens international debt places on them, and look to that biblical time of jubilee when debts are remitted and justice prevails. And they look, in these times and on this earth, for a kingdom and a power that are God's alone, and not the ones under which they live. This book offers resources for the "unpoor" in the churches of the world to explore how we can join the poor in their prayers.

From Where Do We Pray?

Prayer is an activity that always happens at a particular place and time and is engaged in by actual people. The meaning of the words we pray will be charged with the weight of our wealth or poverty, the place we live, the group we belong to, the schooling we have received, and the political beliefs we cherish—whether they are conscious or not. We can only pray from the place we are really standing, and not from some "pious" or abstract space separate from the real world.

If we are not praying for real food, we likely live in a place that is relatively protected; but it is becoming increasingly difficult for us not to know about the world's pain and the urgent need for change. Militarization, poverty, crippling debt, environmental damage are repeatedly brought to our attention. And it is increasingly and uncomfortably obvious that it is not just a question of stark contrasts within the world—*their* deprivation and *our* comfort. Rather, the contrasting positions are deeply connected with each other. We are called on not simply to give generously out of our abundance to those who happen to be less fortunate than ourselves, but to recognize that we too are diminished and wounded, because the world is arranged as it is; and that we also need actively to seek its transformation.

How Do We Pray?

An awareness of the stark contrasts within the world and their interconnectedness can affect our prayers in various ways. It is common to begin the move from a self-satisfied prayer for "them" and "their problems" by adopting one of the following unhelpful stances:

• The path of guilt and paralyzing depression. This kind of prayer catalogues the woes of the poor in infinite, gloomy detail, and also our guilt and failure in allowing or causing them. Prayers like these read as confessions of persons who have no hope of forgiveness. Some of us may derive a kind of bleak satisfaction from this endless rehearsal of our guilt, but it seldom inspires energetic action.

• The path of frenzied programs for action. This prayer is often a manifesto delivered over the congregation's bowed but probably irritated heads, and it is a campaign document with a cursory address to God at the beginning and end. It doesn't assist worship, and is of doubtful value even for campaigning.

• The path of praying as if we were the poor. It is rightly observed that prayers written by actual poor people, or by those closest to them, seldom resemble either of the above. Spoken from the midst of repression, fear, and hunger, they *don't* tend to catalogue horrors (though they show awareness of them), and they *do* often ring with hope, assurance, and confidence in the power of God. Something of the contrast emerges within the material that follows; on the whole, it is not the poor but the "unpoor" who have a tendency to despair when they set the gospel alongside the world's realities. When the poorest communities do the same, they experience hope, because, as a French-speaking priest put it: "Dans L'Evangile c'est comme chez nous" (The Gospel is the story of how we live).

So it is tempting for us to rush into singing the songs of the oppressed as if we could indeed quite simply make their words our own. Sometimes we can, but not simply. We should feel uneasy with a lusty singing of the triumph songs of the poor when we have no right to triumphalism, given where we are standing and which side we've taken. To pretend that we *are* the poor may give us the feeling of occupying the high moral ground we naively assume is theirs, but it doesn't assist either worship or action because it is untruthful.

Much harder, but in the end more hopeful, is to seek solidarity with the poor. Solidarity means truthfully recognizing the place we stand in, while really seeing theirs; and then, with love and honesty and commitment, exploring the connections between us and working together for change. For us, it means facing the complexity and ambivalence of where we are placed, as Christians living in the rich world who want to pray in solidarity with poor. It will entail acknowledging both our participation in sin and our own woundedness. It will require repentance ("metanoia"—a change of stance in relation to the evil that seeks to surround us). But it will also release us to share in a passionate desire for change in the structures of the world—*for our sake too*. We will recognize a struggle and find joy, forgiveness, and salvation as we join it. The poor ask not for patronage but solidarity:

> If you have come to help me, then you are wasting your time. But if you have come because your liberation is bound up with mine, then let us work together.
> Lilla Watson, Australian aboriginal

It is this principle of solidarity and connection in prayer that has shaped the selection of material in this book. Both contrition and intercession are important, but we have tried to avoid futile breast-beating or endless lists of information. Rather, these are resources for a way of praying that recognizes ourselves as members of one world and partners with the poor. It is to pray so that our imagination is touched and our deep desire for change is released.

Why Do We Pray?

We offer worship resources because we believe that prayer not only nourishes commitment, but is itself a crucial form of action for change. There have always been Christians who have tried to hold together struggle and contemplation, however costly, and we seek to be part of that tradition. Prayer is *performative*. When we come together to pray we rightly pray "beyond ourselves"—placing ourselves within a vision of a different world, and so making ourselves part of the process that will bring about those promises. And we place ourselves, with our sisters and brothers, within the hands of God—not merely in our own desperate strivings.

To Whom Do We Pray?

To pray is a significant action because it involves explicitly naming and binding ourselves to what we most value. In doing this we give ourselves the opportunity to stand apart from the values we are unwittingly soaked in, the way of life we implicitly "worship" without reflection or pause. Prayer leaves space for God to reach us as we grope for words that express whom we really choose to praise or whom we want to learn to praise.

It is fatally easy for us to address a "God" who simply reflects our own un-thought-out values and expectations. In the doxology of the Lord's Prayer we recognize that it is to God alone that authority and power and glory belong, and not to human arrangements for control: superior wealth, social status, or military force. Yet, by continuing to pray to a God who seems, as the "Almighty," to have precisely that kind of power, we put ourselves in danger of blessing (or at least seeing no objection to) systematic arrangements for international trade, financial dealing, and military control that impoverish and endanger those with the least power over their own lives.

St. Paul's understanding of the shocking and redemptive nature of the gospel message is that it proclaims a God whose use and choice of power contradicts all the wisdom of the world. Paul asserts that what we preach is deliberate and God-given "folly" (1 Corinthians 1:21). "Christ the power of God and the wisdom of God" is the one who shared the shameful death of a slave, and therefore speaks to us of a God who chooses to be present in what is most "low and despised." It is this gospel that is the hope of the poor, in the contemporary world as much as in Paul's time, and this hope is reflected in the language and imagery of many of the prayers that follow. To pray "Wake up little baby God" (p. 41) is to acknowledge that God wears the swaddling clothes of the poor and not the robes of Herod.

The Prayers

These prayers have been chosen with the assistance of a group representing different faith traditions and cultures. We have sought a balance between prayers from developed and underdeveloped countries, but have tried to ensure that the words that come from our less developed partners can genuinely be prayed in our context too.

The materials have been selected and arranged according to the broad seasons of the church's liturgical year. The group that helped to gather the prayers spent a whole year reflecting on how the traditional themes of each season spoke to, and were illuminated by, a concern to strengthen the poor. We organized a series of days of reflection to explore this more deeply; some of the insights that emerged are described in the short introductions to each section of the book.

We found that the traditional themes and stories of the church's year spring to life — sometimes in unexpected ways — when they touch the world in which we live. And we learned that praying for the "bread of tomorrow" is not an optional interest for the church, suitable only for certain times of year. It is central to the church.

Using These Prayers

The prayers are intended for use in public worship in a variety of settings, as well as for private use; however, not all will be suitable for every kind of gathering, because there is a wide range of formal and informal styles of prayer. Different churches require quite different worship resources. Some need material that is clearly shaped so that it will fit a recognizable place in a regular liturgy, as a collect, a set of intercessions, a eucharistic prayer, and so on. Others want more loosely shaped material that the worship leader can place according to the theme of the service. Still others have a tradition of free prayer that is uneasy with the fixed, written word, and worship leaders will want to use this material only for their own preparation and reflection. It is important in any case not to "pack" a service with unfamiliar words, however striking or instructive, and this caution applies especially to prayers that have some of the density and economy of poetry. Space and silence should be included so that the words used on a particular occasion do not lose their force and vividness. Space and silence are also an integral part of worship.

Because of the variety of worship needs, I have not ordered the material too firmly by type of prayer, but only by the season of the church's year. Even this grouping is to be regarded only as a general guide; you may well find a prayer under Lent that you want to use in Advent, and so forth. But in order to assist the process of choosing a particular type of prayer (contrition, intercession, and so forth), I have included an index with cross-references (p. 169) by type of prayer. The book is not intended to be an exhaustive compendium of resources, but a contribution to a fresh way of praying.

The only essential piece of guidance about use of the material is this: However moving, beautiful, or trenchant are the words offered here, if they are prayed only as an alternative to doing anything concrete about poverty, or as a distraction from such action, or so as to veil how our churches actually stand in solidarity with those who benefit from the continuing poverty of many, then they are misused and will become a danger to the health of our souls.

CALL TO PRAYER

[1]

Come to this table
   to meet the living God,
      love indescribable and beyond our imagining
         yet closer than our own breathing.
Come to this table
   to meet the risen Christ,
      flesh of our flesh, bone of our bone,
         God-with-us, embodied in our living.
Come to this table
   to meet the life-giving Spirit,
      interpreting our search for truth and justice,
         breathing into us renewing power.
Come to find, to meet, to hold
   the living, loving God
      made new for us in bread and wine.

Jan Berry, England, 1990

[2]

Come to the living God,
         Come to stand alongside the poor.
         Come to struggle with those who seek freedom.
         Come to resist all that offends God's justice.
Come to the living, disturbing God.

Jan Berry, England, 1990

ADVENT

The powerful traditional themes of Advent take on a new depth when we include in our prayers an awareness of the forces that keep people poor, and the very concrete hopes for change that give people strength to go on.

It is a season characterized by outrageous promise. One prayer announces: "Those who can't speak will shout" (p. 20), and we know that this includes not only those individuals who suffer speech defects, or are temperamentally shy, but all of those whose voices are discounted, whose protests are unheard, whose wisdom is ignored, because they are thought not to matter. Another litany anchors its startling hope in the truth of biblical promises, declaring, in the teeth of the evidence: "It is not true that we are simply victims of the powers of evil who seek to rule the world." (p. 31)

For in Advent we are especially conscious of the powers of darkness, into which we want the light of Christ to come. For the poor, these are experienced with great immediacy as hunger, disease, military repression, and inescapable debt. For ourselves, more distant from bodily needs and danger, it is often possible to avoid knowing these things and our own part in "all that kills life" for the poor. But because we refuse to know, we find ourselves engulfed in a sort of formless fear and indifference that invades our communal life inside and outside the churches.

This awareness leads to a sense of longing for salvation. Advent is a time of urgent invocation, of crying for God to come and set us free. Our society is characterized by a certain kind of insatiable wanting, and yet the proliferation of consumer goods for those who can afford them (especially noticeable in the weeks before Christmas) does nothing to satisfy our sense of need. Instead of simply condemning this kind of materialism, perhaps we need in the churches to learn from the poor and reclaim prayer as desire—real desire for that justice "in this time, in this world" (p. 32) that will make all of us whole.

Longing for God to come in our world is paralleled by apprehension as to what that coming might mean for us. Light that will comfort and warm in the darkness may also expose what we would rather be hidden or unknown. For the promise of "God with us" may be experienced either as grace or judgment. As the parable of the Sheep and the Goats in Matthew 25 (a traditional Advent reading) makes clear, our very salvation depends on our response to the poor, in whom God waits to be recognized. It is a time of crisis when our material choices about engagement in the world, and not simply our professed beliefs or worship practices, are decisive.

But our sense of urgency is balanced by the requirement to wait—to wait on the timing of God, which we can neither predict nor force. And the poor of the world have much to teach us about waiting—waiting with hope, purpose, and active preparation for change; waiting without falling into despair. For activists it may be hard but necessary to thank God for "the darkness of waiting" (p. 22), and for what we learn "through failing where we hoped to succeed" (p. 15).

In all, Advent is a time of preparation, a time to pray for the enlarging of our hearts that will allow us to know ourselves as part of one world with the poor; a time to pray for that opening of our eyes that we both long for and fear. A middle-class Filipina nun has spoken about her difficulty in facing and knowing about the repression suffered by the majority of her people, for "the cost of awareness is anguish" (Sister Mary John Mananzan). If we want to avoid such awareness, we should certainly not engage in anything as dangerous as prayer. Yet beyond it, we may find a welcome that surprises our guilt with its grace.

A Prayer for Advent

Let us open our hearts to receive
the grace of this Advent season,
which is Christ himself,
whom God our Father has revealed
to the entire world.
Where God is born, hope is born.
Where God is born, peace is born.
And where peace is born,
re is no longer room for hatred and for war.
God alone can save us and free us
from the many forms of evil
and selfishness in our midst.
et us welcome into our lives God's mercy,
which Jesus Christ has bestowed on us,
so that we in turn can show mercy
to our brothers and sisters.
In this way, we will make peace grow!

—Pope Francis

Passanisi Family ....…...Memorial Mass
vard, Josephine & Judy Fitzgerald Memorial

cember 4th

rles Anastasia .... 2nd Anniversary

ley Judge .... 5th Anniversary

icent Fahy .... Memorial Mass

San Damiano Cross Prayer

"Most High glorious God, bring light to the darkness of my heart. Give me right faith, certain hope, and perfect charity, insight, and wisdom , so I can always observe Thy holy and true command. Amen."

2:1-5/Ps 122:1-9/Rom 13:11
7-44

4:2-6/Ps 122/Mt 8:5-11

11:1-10/Ps 72/Lk 10:21-24

: Rom 10:9-18/Ps 23/Mt

Is 26:1-6/Ps 118/Mt 7:21, 24-27

9:17-24/Ps 27/Mt 9:27-31

s 30:19-21, 23-26/Ps 147/Mt 9:35--10:1, 5a, 6-8

y: Is 11:1-10/Ps 72/Rom 15:4-9/Mt 3:1-12

THE WORD OF GOD

[1]

Come humbly, Holy Child,
stir in the womb
of our complacency;
shepherd our vision
of the little we need
for abundant living.

Come humbly, Holy Spirit,
to whisper through the leaves
in the garden of our ignorance,
exposing our blindness
to children dying,
hungry and in pain.

Come humbly, Holy Light,
pierce our lack of generosity and love,
scattering our dark fear
of living freely in your way,
poured out in wanton service.

Come humbly, Holy Wisdom,
cry through the empty streets
of our pretence to care,
that the face of the poor
will be lifted up,
for holy is your name.

Come humbly, Holy God,
be born into our rejoicing.
Come quickly, humble God,
and reign.

A Mothers' Union Day on *Magnificat*, Durham, England, 1989
Proverbs 8; John 1; 1 Corinthians 1:17-28

[2]

When I'm down and helpless
When lies are reigning
When fear and indifference are growing
May your kingdom come.

When joy is missing
When love is missing
and unbelief is growing
May your kingdom come.

To the sick and lonely
To the imprisoned and tortured
May your kingdom come.

Into the churches
Into our praying, into our singing
May your kingdom come.

Into our hearts
Into our hands, into our eyes
May your kingdom come. Soon!

> Czech litany
> *With All God's People*, World Council of Churches, 1989
> Matthew 6:9-13

[3]

You keep us waiting.
You, the God of all time,
want us to wait
for the right time in which to discover
who we are, where we must go,
who will be with us, and what we must do.
So thank you . . . for the waiting time.

You keep us looking.
You, the God of all space,
want us to look in the right and wrong places
for signs of hope,
for people who are hopeless,
for visions of a better world that will appear
among the disappointments of the world we know.
So thank you . . . for the looking time.

You keep us loving.
You, the God whose name is love,
want us to be like you —
to love the loveless and the unlovely and the unlovable;
to love without jealousy or design or threat;
and, most difficult of all,
to love ourselves.
So thank you . . . for the loving time.

And in all this,
you keep us.
Through hard questions with no easy answers;
through failing where we hoped to succeed
and making an impact when we felt we were useless;
through the patience and the dreams and the love of
        others;
and through Jesus Christ and his Spirit,
you keep us.
So thank you . . . for the keeping time,
and for now,
and for ever,
Amen.

Iona Community Worship Book, 1988
Psalms 27, 40, 62, 63; Isaiah 25:1-9, 40:28-31

[4]

Come God
Come with the frightened
Come with the poor
Come with the children
Come with those who have always been your friends
Come and lead us where you are living
and show us what you want us to do.

A Mothers' Union Day on *Magnificat,* Durham, England, 1989
Luke 9:46-48, 10:21

[5]

Who will set us free?
Who else can set us free?

Refrain: Jesus, Jesus, we're waiting,
we're waiting for you.
You said you'd be coming,
you said you'd be coming.
Don't let us hope for nothing,
don't let us hope for nothing.

Who will open our eyes?
Who else can open our eyes?

Who will be our light?
Who else can be our light?

Who will give us life?
Who else can give us life?

Bernardo Maria Perez, Philippines
Sound the Bamboo, Asian Institute for Liturgy and Music, 1990
Romans 6:18; Galatians 5:1

[6]

If we have worshiped you as a relic from the past, a
  theological concept, a religious novelty, but not as a
  living God:
Lord, forgive us.

If we have confused your will with our understanding of it,
  if we have preferred divergence to unity:
Lord, forgive us.

If we have heard stories of struggle, with no intention of
  sharing the burden or pain:
Lord, forgive us.

If we have identified the misuse of power, but failed to
  prophesy against it, and refused to empower the
  weak:
Lord, forgive us.

If we have sung songs in praise of your creation, while
  defiling the goodness of the earth:
Lord, forgive us.

**O God, show mercy to those who have no one else to
  turn to.**

The Lord says: I will bring my people back to me, I will
  love them with all my heart. No longer am I angry
  with them. I will be to the people like rain in a dry
  land.
This is the promise of God.
Amen. Thanks be to God.

National Council of Churches of the Philippines,
14th Biennial Convention Resource Book, 1989
Psalm 72:6; Isaiah 1:12-17, 24:13-14; Hosea 11:1-9

[7]

All: In the awesome name of God,
      in the victorious name of Jesus,
      in the mysterious name of the Spirit,
      we acknowledge our God
      and we wait;
      we are still
      we are silent
      and we wait.

                                    A brief silence

V1: We wait for the sounds of God
     and the sounds of the sacrament:
     the breaking of bread
     and gushing of wine
     the pain of sorrow
     and the pulse of hope
     the echo of our name
     and the bread in our teeth
     a cup on our lips
     and breathing at our side
     as we wait for the sounds of God
     the breaking of bread
     and the gushing of wine.

                                    A brief silence

V2: We hear sounds in the distance:
     the vibration of human lives
     the crackle of fear
     and the murmur of distrust
     the scramble for rice
     and the tearing of garbage
     the shuffle of withered limbs
     and the sigh of rich tourists
     the growl of empty bodies
     and the splash of spent blood

the breaking of the bread
and the gushing of the wine.

A brief silence

V1: We hear the snarl of a bullet
and the snap of a trigger
the sudden yell of unseen mines
the cough of smoking ruins
the whisper of desolation
and the silence of a lifeless field
the breaking of the bread
and the gushing of the wine.

A brief silence

V2: We hear the bleating of the lamb
and the breaking of the womb
the death of the lamb
and the breaking of the tomb
a word that was healing
and a God that was feeling
in the breaking of the bread
and the gushing of the wine.

A brief silence

ALL: And we will wait for the bursting of joy
and the glow of children's faces
and the dancing of willows
and the surprise of open lives
the shout of mountains
and the laughter of a second birth
the leap of our spirit
and the swirl of celebration
in the breaking of the bread
and the gushing of the wine.

Garry Trompf
Your Will Be Done, Christian Conference of Asia Youth, 1984
Isaiah 9:2-7; John 3:3-8; Revelation 7:13-17, 21:1-6

[8]

The desert will sing and rejoice
and the wilderness blossom with flowers;
all will see the Lord's splendor,
see the Lord's greatness and power.
Tell everyone who is anxious:
Be strong and don't be afraid.
The blind will be able to see;
the deaf will be able to hear;
the lame will leap and dance;
those who can't speak will shout.
They will hammer their swords into ploughs
and their spears into pruning-knives;
the nations will live in peace;
they will train for war no more.
This is the promise of God;
God's promise will be fulfilled.

Iona Community Worship Book, 1988
Isaiah 35; Micah 4:1-4

[9]

God, our hope and our desire,
we wait for your coming
as a woman longs for the birth,
the exile for her home,
the lover for the touch of his beloved,
and the humble poor for justice.

Janet Morley, England
Christian Aid
John 16:21-22

[10]

Today I look into my own heart
and all around me, and I sing the song of Mary.

My life praises the Lord my God,
who is setting me free.
God has remembered me, in my humiliation and distress!
From now on, those who rejected and ignored me
will see me and call me happy,
because of the great things God is doing
in my humble life.
God's name is completely different from the other names
    in this world;
  from one generation to another
  God was on the side of the oppressed.
As on the day of the Exodus, God is stretching out
a mighty arm to scatter the oppressors
with all their evil plans.
God has brought down mighty kings
from their thrones
and has lifted up the despised;
and so God will do today.
God has filled the exploited with good things,
and sent the exploiters away with empty hands;
and so God will do today.
God's promise to our mothers and fathers remains new
    and fresh to this day.
Therefore the hope for liberation
which is burning in me
will not be extinguished.
God will remember me, here now and beyond the grave.

Zephania Kameeta, Namibia
Why O Lord?, World Council of Churches, 1986
Luke 1:46-53

[11]

God of the poor,
we long to meet you
yet almost miss you;
we strive to help you
yet only discover our need.
Interrupt our comfort
with your nakedness;
touch our possessiveness
with your poverty,
and surprise our guilt
with the grace of your welcome
    in Jesus Christ. Amen.

Janet Morley, England
God with Us, Christian Aid
Matthew 25:31-46

[12]

For the darkness of waiting
of not knowing what is to come
of staying ready and quiet and attentive,
we praise you, O God:

**For the darkness and the light
are both alike to you.**

For the darkness of staying silent
for the terror of having nothing to say
and for the greater terror
of needing to say nothing,
we praise you, O God:

**For the darkness and the light
are both alike to you.**

For the darkness of loving
in which it is safe to surrender
to let go of our self-protection
and to stop holding back our desire,
we praise you, O God:

**For the darkness and the light
are both alike to you.**

For the darkness of choosing
when you give us the moment
to speak, and act, and change,
and we cannot know what we have set in motion, but we
    still have to take the risk,
we praise you, O God:

**For the darkness and the light
are both alike to you.**

For the darkness of hoping
in a world which longs for you,
for the wrestling and laboring of all creation
for wholeness and justice and freedom,
we praise you, O God:

**For the darkness and the light
are both alike to you.**

Janet Morley, England
All Desires Known, Women in Theology and Movement
for the Ordination of Women, 1988
Psalm 139; Romans 8:18-25

[13]

O God:
Enlarge my heart
that it may be big enough to receive the greatness of
    your love.
Stretch my heart
that it may take into it all those who with me around the
    world
believe in Jesus Christ.
Stretch it
that it may take into it all those who do not know him,
but who are my responsibility because I know him.
And stretch it
that it may take in all those who are not lovely in my eyes,
and whose hands I do not want to touch;
through Jesus Christ, my savior. Amen.

Prayer of an African Christian
With All God's People, World Council of Churches, 1989
Luke 10:25-37

[14]

Have you not heard about him,
O my brothers?
Do you not know about him,
O my sisters?
He was a carpenter.
The wood yielded to his hands.
His yokes were easy upon the ox's neck,
and sweat was upon his brow.
He cared for the beggar and the dog
that licked the beggar's sores.
He brought sight to the blind
and healed the leper.
He cured the diseased in mind
and gave them new life.

He can give you life that is as bread
to your hungry bellies.
He can give you life that is as hours
spent away from your desk.

The hearts that are his
will clear the way and build the road
that is gentle even to crippled feet.
Let him lead us.

Chandran Devanesen, India
"Christ of the Indian Road"
Morning Noon and Night, CMS, 1976
Matthew 11:2-6

[15]

Open my eyes that they may see
the deepest needs of people;
move my hands that they may feed the hungry;
touch my heart that it may bring warmth to the
    despairing;
teach me the generosity that welcomes strangers;
let me share my possessions to clothe the naked;
give me the care that strengthens the sick;
make me share in the quest to set the prisoner free.
In sharing our anxieties and our love,
our poverty and our prosperity,
we partake of your divine presence.

Canaan Banana, Zimbabwe
With All God's People, World Council of Churches, 1989
Matthew 25:31-46

[16]

When I come in the guise
of the needy, the helpless,
the cold and the hungry,
the stranger, the lonely,
will you look away?
What will you do?
What will you say?

When I come close to home
in the need of your neighbor,
at times inconvenient,
in places and faces
that mask and conceal me . . .
What will you do?
What will you say?

When I come in the message
of prophet and preacher,
in truths inescapable
or words which dismay,
will you listen to me
and give me a welcome?
What will you do?
What will you say?

When, face to face
at the end of the journey,
we look at each other,
will you look away?
What will I do?
What will I say?

Kenneth Carveley
All Year Round, British Council of Churches, 1988
Exodus 3:2-7; Matthew 25:31-46; Luke 9:23-26,
16:19-31

[17]

The poor of the world are thirsty
for justice and for peace,
their journey is unending
till hate and oppression cease.

The Lord of Heaven is thirsty
for justice and for peace;
the Lord's battle is unending
till hate and oppression cease.

Pastoral Team of Bambamarca, Peru
Vamos Caminando: A Peruvian Catechism, Orbis Books, 1985
Isaiah 55

[18]

Open up the way for the people!
Prepare the road! Prepare the road!
Make it clean, leave no stones on it!
Raise high the banner, that all may see it!
Say to my people, "Look, your Savior comes."
They will call you the holy people,
the people whom the Lord has freed.

Pastoral Team of Bambamarca, Peru
Vamos Caminando: A Peruvian Catechism, Orbis Books, 1985
Isaiah 35:10, 40:3-5; Luke 3:4-6

[19]

Come to the world!
Yes, God the Creator, come!
Things are not as you created them in the beginning.
Come, God, for it is your help we need in the world.

Peace of mind,
Yes, that's what everyone wants.
Our need, please, God, is true peace in the world.
Peace of mind,
Yes, that's what everyone prays for.

What is our state in the world?
Come and see how our people are destroying the world,
without seeking what is in your heart,
without seeking what is in your mind . . .

Yes, if we seek peace,
God will grant us peace . . .
It is peace that encourages our heart;
and making peace
that is the guarantee of hope.

Ikoli Harcourt Whyte, Nigeria
All Year Round, British Council of Churches, 1987
Luke 1:76-79, 19:41-44

[20]

Holy Lord,
some day the burden of today's toil —
the goings and comings,
the successes and failures,
the hopes and near despairs —
will all be transformed
into blessed reality!

Hope will be no more . . .
I reach the point of near absurdity:
of thanking you that I live
during the difficult phase
in which hope is still
the beginning of the beginning of the day!
Day is still struggling,
and has many struggles ahead,
to be born.

From the mingled light and shadow
of hope
I greet you, Lord God.

A Basic Christian Community in the Philippines

[21]

O God of all youth, we pray to you:
We are young people, and we want to celebrate life!
We cry out against all that kills life:
   hunger, poverty, unemployment, sickness,
   repression, individualism, injustice.
We want to announce fullness of life:
   work, education, health, housing,
   bread for all.
We want communion, a world renewed,
We hope against hope.
With the Lord of history we want to make all things new.

A group of Brazilian young people
With All God's People, World Council of Churches, 1989
Deuteronomy 30:19; Isaiah 44:19;
2 Corinthians 5:17; Revelation 21:5

[22]

My soul magnifies the Lord,
and in God my heart exults:
Salidum salidummay,
in sinalidumiway. Ay ay salidummay.

Favored look God cast on me,
shadowed me so tenderly,
generations then will see
deep things God works silently. *Ay ay salidummay.*

To God-fearing souls God shows,
and sure mercy God bestows;
and the strength of God's right arm
scatters all the proud who swarm. *Ay ay salidummay.*

All enthroned God will bring down,
and the lowly God does crown;
hungry ones God fills with good,
but the rich God brings to rue. *Ay ay salidummay.*

So the promise from of old
comes to life, does not grow cold;
promise made to Abraham and Sarah
bears its fruit—your kingdom come. *Ay ay salidummay.*

"Blessed Mary" all saints say;
"your consent has paved the way.
Our salvation is now done,
by the coming God the Son." *Ay ay salidummay*

Henry Kiley, Philippines
Sound the Bamboo, Asian Institute
for Liturgy and Music, 1990
Luke 1:46-53

[23]

We are called to proclaim the truth . . . And let us believe:
It is not true that this world and its people are
doomed to die and to be lost.
**This is true: I have come that they may have life in all
its abundance.**

It is not true that we must accept inhumanity and
discrimination, hunger and poverty, death and
destruction.
**This is true: the deaf hear, the dead are raised to life,
the poor are hearing the good news.**

It is not true that violence and hatred should have the last
word, and that war and destruction have come to
stay forever.
**This is true: death shall be no more, neither shall there
be mourning nor crying nor pain any more.**

It is not true that we are simply victims of the powers of
evil who seek to rule the world.
**This is true: the Lord whom we seek will suddenly
come to the temple; and the Lord is like a refiner's
fire.**

It is not true that our dreams of liberation, of human
dignity, are not meant for this earth and for this
history.
**This is true: it is already time for us to wake from
sleep. For the night is far gone, the day is at hand.**

> Adapted from an address by Allan Boesak, South Africa
> World Council of Churches, 1983
> John 10:10; Matthew 11:5; Revelation 21:4;
> Malachi 3:1-2; Romans 13:11-12

[24]

All the broken hearts
shall rejoice;
all those who are heavy laden,
whose eyes are tired
and do not see,
shall be lifted up
to meet with
the motherly healer.
The battered souls and bodies
shall be healed;
the hungry
shall be fed;
the imprisoned
shall be free;
all her earthly children
shall regain joy
in the reign
of the just and loving one
coming for you
coming for me
in this time
in this world.

Sun Ai Park, Korea
In God's Image, April 1986
Isaiah 25:4-9, 40:1-11, 61, 65:17-25; Matthew 11:28-30

CHRISTMAS/EPIPHANY

Christmas is about scandal. Poets throughout generations have meditated on the astonishing paradoxes involved in incarnation, whereby God relinquishes power and is found in the helpless and vulnerable body of a baby, unprotected from human poverty and danger. This defies our imagination. We find it easier to sentimentalize Christmas when we pray.

The experience of millions of the poorest in our world, though, is identical to that first Christmas story; and to pray in solidarity with them is to experience the immediacy of a scandal that is repeated again and again in shanty town, barrio, and cardboard city. Our love must be grounded and particular — as God's is — and not some neutral and vague seasonal goodwill that is really inattentive and self-important. The Asian theologian C. S. Song says of incarnation:

Love is essentially gravity-bound. When it becomes gravity-free, it is no longer love. It turns into a force that repels. It is hate, rejection, alienation, condemnation and death. But God is drawn to the world through a gravity-bound love. (*Tell Us Our Names,* Orbis Books, 1984)

In praying to a God who has chosen to be bound by gravity, and all the constraints of human poverty, we offer our own loving to be remade like God's love.

For the poor, that love can be the source of their resilience and strength. The Word made flesh is experienced in their own vision and struggle for liberation. Like the shepherds who were the first to see the Christchild in the manger, they may "look level-eyed into the face of God" (p. 45).

Some of us may find we cannot bear to do this. Yet if we also can shed some of our privilege and pride, and recognize our own emptiness, we may discover that "all who kneel and hold out their hands are unstintingly fed" (p. 44).

The Christmas season is followed by Epiphany, which takes its themes from the journey of the magi, the (presumably) rich and articulate foreigners who undertook a journey of discovery to search for the Christ. There is, in this season, a sense of trying to see more clearly, of being open to "epiphany" — the showing forth of God in unexpected places. Several of the prayers and meditations explore the idea that something new is being shown to those who move away from familiar ground in order to have their eyes opened. This may be unsettling, but it is also full of unforeseen delight and grace.

The journey of those "wise men" seems to be a paradigm for those of us who want, even from a position of privilege, to learn from the context of the poor and offer what gifts we can. But what we can miss is the end of the story — brutal military repression, set in motion unintentionally by the foreigners whose well-meaning arrival in the wrong place aroused suspicions and created new danger. The travellers were suddenly transformed from examples into object-lessons of mistaken patronage:

> We call them wise
> and I had always thought of them that way
> respecting the pilgrimage of anyone
> who sees a star and follows it
> to his or her discomfiting —
> being prepared to change.
> And yet,
> in following their star, the star
> that was to lead them to
> enlargement of the soul (their own) . . .

they blundered mightily, and set in train
the massacre of many innocents.
Naive and foolish men they were, not wise,
to go and ask of Herod
"Where's your rival,
where is he who might unseat you?"

I wonder if,
back in their own countries,
for all that they themselves were born again,
they heard the voice of Rachel
weeping for her children
refusing to be comforted
because they were no more?

Kate Compston

If for us prayer is confined to the realm of an internal pilgrimage, any amount of apparent spiritual insight is irrelevant if we simultaneously "blunder mightily" in our understanding of how power is abused and how we ourselves are involved. Prayer that is deaf to the "voice of Rachel" has missed the Epiphany. Prayer is only truly "contemplation" when it enables us to see all that is to be seen, including the violent realities we are normally *not* prepared to contemplate.

CHRISTMAS

[1]

Holy Child of Bethlehem,
    whose parents found no room in the inn,
    we pray for all who are homeless.

Holy Child of Bethlehem,
    born in a stable,
    we pray for all who live in poverty.

Holy Child of Bethlehem,
    rejected stranger,
    we pray for all who are lost, alone,
    all who cry for loved ones.

Holy Child of Bethlehem,
    whom Herod sought to kill,
    we pray for all who live with danger,
    all who are persecuted.

Holy Child of Bethlehem,
    a refugee in Egypt,
    we pray for all who are far from their homes.

Holy Child of Bethlehem,
    in you God was pleased to dwell,
    help us, we pray, to see the divine image
    in people everywhere.

> David Blanchflower, England
> *All Year Round,* British Council of Churches, 1987
> Matthew 2:13-23; Luke 2:1-20

[2]

From the cowardice that dares not face new truth
From the laziness that is contented with half-truth
From the arrogance that thinks it knows all truth,
Good Lord, deliver me.

Prayer from Kenya
Morning, Noon and Night, ed. John Carden, SMC, 1976

[3]

Helpless God as child and crucified,
laid in a cradle and cradled on a cross:
help us discern in your submission
not weakness but the passionate work of love.

You tell us you are poor in every age:
naked, hungry, and without a home.

Help us in your poor cradle of today
to see what is of you and what is not:
that suffering does not often save,
or helplessness redeem our sorry lives.
And so forbid us sing when we should weep.

Yet come to us and all of ours,
O child of Mary and of God,
in all the poor who saw you first,
and laughed with you, and heard you well.
And now run back from nowhere with their news,
to plant their seeds of hope in our dry ground.

Michael H. Taylor, England
Christian Aid
Matthew 25:31-46; Mark 14:7; Luke 2:8-18

[4]

Choosing God

Choosing to let your child be born in poverty
and of doubtful parentage

Choosing an occupied country with unstable rulers

Choosing the risk of his dying in a dirty stable
after a long journey by a pregnant teenager

Choosing to let him grow up poor, and in danger,
and misunderstood by those who loved him

Choosing God
we doubt the wisdom of your choices then,
and we doubt them now,
while the rich are still full
and it is the poor who get sent empty away

Help us, lest we in our anger or ignorance
choose to walk another way.

A Mothers' Union Day on *Magnificat*, Durham, England 1989
Matthew 2; Mark 3:21-35; Luke 1:46-53; 1 Corinthians 1:18-29

[5]

Here I am
one small voice;
here I am
one young soul.
Let me join your world,
enjoy your world,
and take it as my own.
I need your love.

Here we are;
take a look at us.
Here we are;
can you see us at all?
All alone and unsure—
can you feel our fears?
Let us share them all with you.

Don't take away my time to be a child:
let me breathe the air with you;
give me room to be and space to see;
lend me a name, a voice to sing my dreams.
Tell me, can I share your world?
Share the world with me—
I am one young dream;
I need your love.

HALAD Review, Philippines, 1990

[6]

God our midwife,
contain in your hands
the breaking of waters,
the blood and din of your birth:
then, through our tears and joy, deliverer,
your wrinkled, infant kingdom may be born.
Amen.

Gill Paterson, England
Christian Aid
Psalm 22:9-10

[7]

The Word, for our sake,
became poverty clothed as the poor
who live off the refuse heap.

The Word, for our sake,
became a sob a thousand times stifled
in the immovable mouth of the child
who dies from hunger.

The Word, for our sake,
became danger in the anguish of the mother
who worries about her son growing into manhood.

The Word cut us deeply in that place of shame:
the painful reality of the poor.

The Word blew its spirit over the dried bones of the
    churches, guardians of silence.

The Word awoke us from the lethargy
which had robbed us of our hope.

The Word became a path in the jungle,
a decision on the farm,
love in women,
unity among workers,
and a Star for those few who can inspire dreams.

The Word became light,
The Word became history,
The Word became conflict,

The Word became indomitable Spirit,
and sowed its seeds
upon the mountain,
near the river
and in the valley,

and those of good will heard the angels sing.

Tired knees were strengthened,
trembling hands were stilled,
and the people who wandered in darkness
saw the light.

The Word became the seed of justice
and we conceived peace.
The Word made justice to rain
and peace came forth from the furrows in the land.
And we saw its glory in the eyes of the poor
transformed into real men and women.

And those who saw the star
opened up for us
the path we now follow.

Julia Esquivel, Guatemala
Threatened with Resurrection,
The Brethren Press, United States, 1982
John 1:14; Luke 2:13-14

[8]

Wake up
little baby God
thousands of children
have been born
just like you
without a roof
without bread
without protection.

Chile, Christmas Card

[9]

Lord, I am blind—
for I am afraid.
Lord, I am blind—
for I do not want to see.
You promise to heal the blind—
and that terrifies me.
I have seen the light—
and I want to close my eyes.
I ask you to shake me,
but I fear being broken.
I ask you to bless me,
but I fear being made whole.

Neill Thew, England
Christian Aid
Isaiah 6:9-10; Matthew 11:2-6

[10]

Will you come and see the light from the stable door?
It is shining newly bright, though it shone before.
It will be your guiding star, it will show you who you are.
Will you hide or decide to meet the light?

Will you step into the light that can free the slave?
It will stand for what is right, it will heal and save.
By the pyramids of greed there's a longing to be freed.
Will you hide or decide to meet the light?

Will you tell about the light in the prison cell?
Though it's shackled out of sight, it is shining well.
When the truth is cut and bruised, and the innocent
    abused,
will you hide or decide to meet the light?

Will you join the hope alight in a young girl's eyes
of the mighty put to flight by a baby's cries?
When the lowest and the least are the foremost at the
    feast,
will you hide or decide to meet the light?

Will you travel by the light of the babe new born?
In the candle lit at night there's a gleam of dawn,
and the darkness all about is too dim to put it out:
will you hide or decide to meet the light?

Brian Wren, England
God with Us, Christian Aid, 1989
Matthew 11:2-15; Luke 1:46-53, 14:15-24;
John 1:4-5, 3:19-21

[11]

This is the day that wise men
And shepherds came to the poor manger,
This is the day of the news
About making easier bent souls.

See the king of anguish and tears
Lying in his cradle
Wrapped with sins' sadness,
Wearing the thorns of the world.

The complicated purpose of love
And God's living workmanship are interwoven
    In the little flesh
        At Christmas.

Gwyn Thomas, Wales
"Ysgyrion Gwaed Gwasg Gee," *Welsh Pilgrim's Manual,*
ed. Brendan O'Malley, Gomer, 1989

[12]

Thank you,
scandalous God,
for giving yourself to the world,
not in the powerful and extraordinary,
but in weakness and the familiar:
in a baby; in bread and wine.

Thank you
for offering, at journey's end, a new beginning;
for setting, in the poverty of a stable,
the richest jewel of your love;
for revealing, in a particular place,
your light for all nations.

Thank you
for bringing us to Bethlehem, House of Bread,
where the empty are filled,
and the filled are emptied;
where the poor find riches,
and the rich recognize their poverty;
where all who kneel and hold out their hands
are unstintingly fed.

Kate Compston, England, 1990
Matthew 2:1-12

[13]

Through Jesus, our greatest treasure,
came an explosion of true love.
He shattered the splendid walls
of the proud fortresses of the world's great ones.
He put his hand in the hand of the weak
and brought peace to humble dwellings.

Gwylim R. Jones, Wales
"Mae Gen i Lyn a cherddi eraill," *Welsh Pilgrim's Manual,*
ed. Brendan O'Malley, Gomer, 1989

[14]

Blessed art thou,
O Christmas Christ,
that thy cradle was so low
that shepherds,
poorest and simplest of earthly folk,
could yet kneel beside it,
and look level-eyed into the face of God.

Anonymous
The Light Shines, Christian Aid Christmas Anthology, 1985
Luke 2:8-20

EPIPHANY

[15]

There is dignity here—
  we will exalt it.
There is courage here—
  we will support it.
There is humanity here—
  we will enjoy it.
There is a universe in every child—
  we will share in it.
There is a voice calling through
  the chaos of our times;
there is a spirit moving across
  the waters of our world;
there is movement,
  a light,
  a promise of hope.
Let them that have eyes to see,
see.
Let them that have ears to hear,
hear.
        But
look not for Armageddon,
nor listen for a trumpet.
Behold, we bring you good tidings of great joy:
the incarnation.

Philip Andrews
"The Song of the Magi," *Suffering and Hope,*
ed. Ron O'Grady and Lee Soo Jin,
Christian Conference of Asia, Singapore, 1976
Genesis 1:2; Mark 4:9, 23, 8:18; Luke 2:10

[16]

O God,
who am I now?
Once, I was secure
  in familiar territory
  in my sense of belonging
unquestioning of
  the norms of my culture
  the assumptions built into my language
  the values shared by my society.

But now you have called me out and away from home
and I do not know where you are leading.
I am empty, unsure, uncomfortable.
I have only a beckoning star to follow.

Journeying God,
pitch your tent with mine
so that I may not become deterred
by hardship, strangeness, doubt.
Show me the movement I must make
  toward a wealth not dependent on possessions
  toward a wisdom not based on books
  toward a strength not bolstered by might
  toward a God not confined to heaven
but scandalously earthed, poor, unrecognized . . .

Help me to find myself
as I walk in others' shoes.

Kate Compston, England, 1990
John 1:14; Hebrews 13:13-14

[17]

We thought we knew where to find you;
we hardly needed a star to guide the way,
just perseverance and common sense;
why do you hide yourself away from the powerful
and join the refugees and outcasts,
calling us to follow you there?
   Wise God, give us wisdom.

We thought we had laid you safe in the manger;
we wrapped you in the thickest sentiment we could find,
and stressed how long ago you came to us;
why do you break upon us in our daily life
with messages of peace and goodwill,
demanding that we do something about it?
   Just and righteous God, give us justice and
   righteousness.

So where else would we expect to find you
but in the ordinary place with the faithful people,
turning the world to your purpose through them.
Bring us to that manger, to that true rejoicing,
which will make wisdom, justice, and righteousness alive
   in us.

Stephen Orchard, England
All the Glorious Names, United Reformed Church
Prayer Handbook, London, 1989
Luke 2:1-20

[18]

"Its outspread wings will fill the breadth of your land,
    O Immanuel."
Where the waters of the river overflow its banks,
I entreat you, O Immanuel,
spread your wings and protect your children from the
    flood!
Where famine yet rages,
I entreat you, O Immanuel,
spread your wings, protect your children from starvation!
Where the butcher's knife sheds the blood of innocents,
I entreat you, O Immanuel,
spread your wings, protect your children
that their corpses shall not cover the wilderness!
O Immanuel, you provide for the birds of the air,
how can you allow humanity, created in your image,
to die on the barren earth?
Abel's blood cried out to you from the earth,
and you sought after him.
Can you then allow the blood of innocents to be shed?
O Immanuel, spread your wings, I entreat you,
fill the breadth of your land
and cover your children who dwell here!

Wang Weifan, China
Lilies of the Field, trans. Janice and Philip Wickeri,
Foundation for Theological Education in South East Asia,
Hong Kong, 1988
Matthew 2:13-18; Isaiah 8:5-8

[19]

Beckoning God—
who called the rich to travel toward poverty,
                    the wise to embrace your folly,
                    the powerful to know their own frailty;
who gave to strangers
                    a sense of homecoming in an alien land
and to stargazers
                    true light and vision as they bowed to earth—
we lay ourselves open to your signs for us.

Stir us with holy discontent over a world
which gives its gifts to those
                    who have plenty already
                    whose talents are obvious
                    whose power is recognized;
and help us
both to share our resources with those who have little
and to receive with humility the gifts they bring to us.

Rise within us, like a star,
and make us restless
till we journey forth
to seek our rest in you.

                    Kate Compston, England, 1990
                    Matthew 2:1-12; 1 Corinthians 1:18-29

[20]

God of gold, we seek your glory:
    the richness that transforms our drabness into color,
    and brightens our dullness with vibrant light;
your wonder and joy at the heart of all life.

God of incense, we offer you our prayer:
    our spoken and unspeakable longings, our questioning
        of truth,
    our searching for your mystery deep within.

God of myrrh, we cry out to you in our suffering:
    the pain of all our rejections and bereavements,
    our baffled despair at undeserved suffering,
    our rage at continuing injustice;
and we embrace you, God-with-us,
in our wealth, in our yearning, in our anger and loss.

Jan Berry, England, 1990
Matthew 2; Job 24:1-12

[21]

My singing heart, my days' doxology, my gold,
    I bring for CELEBRATION.

My stillness, my glimpses of serenity, my frankincense,
    I bring for MEDITATION.

My brokenness, my tears of rage and sorrow, my myrrh,
    I bring for SACRIFICE.

Kate Compston, England, 1990

[22]

What can we bring to your sufficiency but our poverty?
What can we bring to your beauty but our wretchedness?
What can we bring to your wholeness but our
    woundedness?

Made poor, wretched and wounded for our sakes,
you welcome us, wherever we are, whatever we bring.

Kate Compston, England, 1990

[23]

When the song of the angels is stilled
when the star in the sky is gone
when the kings and princes are home
when the shepherds are back with their flocks
the work of Christmas begins:
to find the lost
to heal the broken
to feed the hungry
to release the prisoner
to rebuild the nations
to bring peace among the people
to make music in the heart.

Howard Thurman, United States
Published on Christmas card *Christmas Begins,*
Fellowship of Reconciliation, New York
Luke 4:16-19

LENT

The season of Lent is a classic time for self-examination within the church's year. Based on the story of Jesus' extended period of temptation in the desert, the image is one of *retreat* from our everyday preoccupations to take stock of the direction of our lives. Unfortunately, it has become popularly associated with "giving things up" — a sort of minor asceticism undertaken for the good of our individual souls. To pray in solidarity with the poor will call us into quite a different desert journey, where Lenten discipline will precisely *not* be a retreat from the desperately disturbing challenges of the world into some private piety.

Rather, it will be an opportunity to explore what is the nature of the promised Reign of God on earth that we long for, and to try and discern, amid various tempting strategies, how we are called to work for it. We shall seek to be contemplatives in the sense of asking for "clear eyes to see the world as it is" (p. 62), and to express sorrow for our part in what is continuingly evil in it.

There are those in our churches who speak seriously about the power of Satan, but tend to mean a personal devil who picks off individuals, one by one. And there are others who are totally embarrassed by such language, and indeed prefer not to mention sin at all, believing that guilt feelings are somehow inherently bad for us. Both views seem naive, especially when compared with what our Christian partners among the poor are saying. They identify as being in the grip of sin not only culpable individuals but also structures that keep whole communities locked in poverty. Paradoxically, truthful recognition of the pervasiveness of evil leads not to despair but to clarity and hope, so that we can affirm the words of Jesus that announce the convincing defeat of evil: "I have seen Satan fall" (p. 67).

Lent is also a time when we are invited to follow Jesus along the journey that brought him to the cross. To consider the nature of that challenge from the perspective of the poor is to let our traditional spiritual metaphors leap into a vivid and raw reality. The confession by Joe Seremane of South Africa, which speaks of hesitation and half-hearted commitment, emerges from a context where drawing back from discipleship is not about boredom or having better things to do with one's time. It is about the real danger of imprisonment or death for "taking seriously the meaning of your cross" (p.76). To seek to stand alongside such fellow Christians is to reassess what we have ever meant by the "cost of discipleship."

It is important that the service that is asked of us, the active engagement of our hands, feet, or voices, is not understood only as a one-way gift. One of the hardest assumptions for Western society to relinquish is the view of ourselves as privileged and generous givers. There is much wisdom we desperately need to receive from those who are in a better position than we are to see the world accurately—if only we could acknowledge our lack: "Pray that I may have the grace to let you be my servant too" (p. 57).

To ally ourselves with the struggle against poverty will be to find ourselves curiously freed. The sheer senselessness of the beatitudes—"Blessed are the poor"—becomes fraught with meaning and joy when spoken by those who have literally nothing to lose. The challenge of Lent, whose cost is not less than everything, turns out to be simultaneously an invitation to a "way of celebration" (p. 78) and a journey undertaken in the best possible company. For to follow the way of Jesus is to join the apparently insignificant "little ones" who will be first in the Reign of God. With them

> We travel with authority
> fearful of none;
> we are sent, opponents of evil,
> heralds of hope (p. 68).

[1]

May it come soon
to the hungry
to the weeping
to those who thirst for your justice,
to those who have waited centuries
for a truly human life.
Grant us the patience
to smooth the way
on which your Kingdom comes to us.
Grant us hope
that we may not weary
in proclaiming and working for it,
despite so many conflicts,
threats and shortcomings.
Grant us a clear vision
that in the hour of our history
we may see the horizon,
and know the way
on which your Kingdom comes to us.

Nicaragua
Windows into Worship, ed. Ron Ingamells, YMCA, 1989
Matthew 5:3-12, 6:9-13

[2]

Our Lord,
who is in us here on earth,
holy is your name
in the hungry
who share their bread and their song.
Your Kingdom come,
which is a generous land
that flows with milk and honey.
Let us do your will,
standing up when all are sitting down,
and raising our voice when all are silent.
You are giving us our daily bread
in the song of the bird and the miracle of the corn.
Forgive us
for keeping silent in the face of injustice,
and for burying our dreams,
for not sharing bread and wine,
love and the land,
among us, now.
Don't let us fall into the temptation
of shutting the door through fear;
of resigning ourselves to hunger and injustice;
of taking up the same arms as the enemy.
But deliver us from evil.

Give us the perseverance and the solidarity
to look for love,
even if the path has not yet been trodden,
even if we fall;
so we shall have known your kingdom
which is being built for ever and ever.
Amen.

Central American Lord's Prayer (shortened)
Matthew 6:9-13; Luke 11:2-4

[3]

Brother, let me be your servant,
let me be as Christ to you;
pray that I may have the grace
to let you be my servant too.

We are pilgrims on a journey,
and companions on the road;
we are here to help each other
walk the mile and bear the load.

I will hold the Christ-light for you
in the night-time of your fear;
I will hold my hand out to you,
speak the peace you long to hear.

I will weep when you are weeping;
when you laugh I'll laugh with you.
I will share your joy and sorrow
till we've seen this journey through.

When we sing to God in heaven
we shall find such harmony,
born of all we've known together
of Christ's love and agony.

Sister, let me be your servant,
let me be as Christ to you;
pray that I may have the grace
to let you be my servant too.

Richard Gillard, United States
Scripture in Song, Kansas City, 1977
John 13:1-14; Romans 12:15; Galatians 6:2

[4]

You seduced me, Lord,
and I was seduced.

You grasped my heart firmly
with the outstretched hand
of the old Indian
who has been dying for centuries
without a roof,
without medicines,
without a doctor,
asking for the bread of justice
at the door of a locked church.

You seduced me, Lord,
and I let myself be seduced.
You have conquered me,
you have been stronger than I.

This is why those who were my friends
are retreating in fear
and close their doors to me.
Because each time
I hear your Word
I must cry out:
Violence and ruin
to those who manufacture
orphans, misery, and death!
How many times
did I wish to close my ears
to your voice,
to harden my heart,
to seal my lips,
to forget forever
the pain of the persecuted,

the helplessness of the outcast,
and the agony of the tortured,
but your pain
was my own
and your love
burned in my heart.

You accompany me,
you weep with my weeping,
and moan during my prayer,
and pour yourself out in my cry.

Because you are
stronger than I,
I have let myself be a captive,
and your love
burns in my heart.

Julia Esquivel, Guatemala
Threatened with Resurrection,
The Brethren Press, United States, 1982
Jeremiah 20:7-13

[5]

Christ, our partner,
you invite us to bear your yoke,
so that sharing in your work,
we may find our real selves
in relationship with you
and with those
we would bring to your friendship.

Myra Birdsall, England
Christian Aid
Matthew 11:28-30

[6]

Kumba Yah, my Lord, Kumba Yah (3)
O Lord Kumba Yah.
Someone's crying Lord, Kumba Yah (3)
O Lord Kumba Yah.

Someone's crying Lord.
The "some" today is not one
but several millions, Lord,
not only men, but mostly women.
There are tears of fear and suffering.
There are tears of strength and resistance.
There are tears of weakness and disappointment.
Women are crying, Lord, redeem the times.

Someone's dying, Lord . . . (3)

Some are dying of hunger and thirst.
Some are dying because there are structures and systems
which crush the poor and alienate the rich.
Some are dying because we forget
to give women fullness of life.
Someone's dying, Lord,
because we are still not prepared to take sides,
to make a choice and be your witnesses.
Women are dying, Lord,
redeem our structures and systems.

Someone's shouting, Lord . . . (3)

Someone's shouting, Lord,
shouting out boldly with courage.
Someone has made a choice—
ready to challenge the oppression,
ready to offer her life

in confidence and commitment
to fight death surrounding us
to fight against the evils
that crucify each other.
Someone's shouting, Lord.
Redeem her and strengthen her hands.

Someone's praying, Lord . . . (3)

Someone's praying, Lord,
we join in praying with tears:
in frustration and weakness,
in strength and endurance,
in confidence and commitment.
We are shouting and wrestling;
we are praying, Lord.
Spur our imagination,
sharpen our will,
touch us to be touched,
renew us to renew your world,
bless us to be a blessing.
We are praying, Lord.
Renew and transform the times.

> *Asian Women Doing Theology,*
> Asian Women's Resource Centre, Hong Kong
> Genesis 32:22-32

[7] A LITANY FOR THE WORLD WE LIVE IN

Voice 1: For exploiter and exploited;
          for persecutor and persecuted;
          for criminal and victim,
          God of perfect love, we pray.

Voice 2: As we pray, remove the fear
          that makes us strident and vengeful,
          and take away the woolliness of thought
          that makes us sentimental.

Voice 1: Give us clear eyes to see the world as it is
          and ourselves and all people as we are;
          but give us hope to go on believing
          in what you intend us all to be.

Voice 2: We pray for children growing up
          with no sense of beauty,
          no feeling for what is good or bad,
          no knowledge of you and your love in Christ.

Voice 1: We pray for men and women who have lost faith
          and given up hope;
          for governments who crush people's spirits,
          and for governments slow to act
          in the cause of justice, freedom, and
                development.

Voice 2: We pray for the whole church and the world,
          giving thanks for your goodness,
          for your love made known in Christ,
          for your truth confirmed in his death and
                resurrection,
          for your promises to us and to all people,
          keeping hope alive.

All: Let us go to our work and into our relationships
        stimulated by hope,
        strengthened by faith,
        directed by love,
        to play our part in the liberation of all people,
        in the name of Jesus Christ our Lord. Amen.

Algoa Regional Council (Eastern Cape, South Africa)
of the United Congregational Church
Cry Justice, John de Gruchy, Orbis Books, 1986
Matthew 5:43-48

[8]

Our God and Lord,
we confess with shame that we have come short of your
    glory.
We have not done what we ought to have done.
We have remained deaf to the cries of those who hurt.
We have remained dumb in the face of evil.
We have allowed the shadow of death to hover over the
    innocently condemned.
We have failed to proclaim with power and conviction
    your liberation for the oppressed.
We repent.
In your grace and mercy, forgive us;
renew us in mind, heart, and spirit,
through Jesus Christ our Lord.
Amen.

Lesley G. Anderson, Panama/United Kingdom
Proverbs 21:13

[9]

O God, you claim me as your partner, respecting me,
trusting me,
tussling with me.
Support me
as I dare to be vulnerable with you,
encourage me
as I dare to take risks with you,
so together we can transform our world.
Amen.

Bridget Rees, England
Christian Aid
Genesis 32:22-32

[10]

"In baptism, Jesus takes the 'solidarity dip,' entering the
    struggles of his people."

Brother Christ,
help us to follow you
deep into the waters of baptism,
to break the chain of past wrongs,
to become fit to face your coming age.
Jesus, our Brother, help us to follow you.

Help us to follow you into the desert,
with you to fast, denying false luxury-values,
refusing the tempting ways of self-indulgence,
the way of success at all costs,
the way of coercive persuasion.
Jesus, our Brother, help us to follow you.

Help us to follow you in untiring ministry
to town and village,
to heal and restore,
to cast out the demonic forces
of greed, resentment, communal hatred,
and self-destructive fears rampant in our lands.
Jesus, our Brother, help us to follow you.

Help us to follow you into the place of quiet retreat,
to intercede for the confused, the despairing, the anxiety-
    driven,
to prepare ourselves for costly service.
Jesus, our Brother, help us to follow you.

Help us to follow you on the road to Jerusalem,
to set our faces firmly against friendly suggestions
to live a safe, expedient life,
to embrace boldly the way of self-offering.
Jesus, our Brother, help us to follow you.

Help us to follow you even to the cross,
to see our hope in your self-spending love,
to die to all within us not born of your love.
Jesus, our Brother, help us to follow you.

Help us to follow you out of the dark tomb,
to share daily in your resurrection life,
to be renewed daily in your image of love,
to serve daily as your new body
being broken for your world.
Jesus, our Brother, help us to follow you.

Adapted by Christopher Duraisingh, India
"A Litany of the Disciples of the Servant,"
Morning Noon and Night, ed. John Carden, CMS, 1976
Matthew 3:13-17, 4:1-11; Mark 1:21-28, 5:1-20, 9:31-38;
Luke 9:53; Romans 6:3-4

[11]

Do not retreat into your private world,
That place of safety, sheltered from the storm,
Where you may tend your garden, seek your soul,
And rest with loved ones where the fire burns warm.

To tend a garden is a precious thing,
But dearer still the one where all may roam,
The weeds of poison, poverty, and war,
Demand your care, who call the earth your home.

To seek your soul it is a precious thing,
But you will never find it on your own,
Only among the clamor, threat, and pain
Of other people's need will love be known.

To rest with loved ones is a precious thing,
But peace of mind exacts a higher cost,
Your children will not rest and play in quiet,
While they still hear the crying of the lost.

Do not retreat into your private world,
There are more ways than firesides to keep warm.
There is no shelter from the rage of life,
So meet its eye, and dance within the storm.

> Kathy Galloway, Scotland, 1989
> (Meter: 10.10.10.10)
> 1 Kings 19:9-18; Luke 12:13-21, 17:19-31

[12]

Let us name what is evil in our world,
and in the name of Jesus proclaim its defeat.

In a world where the rich are protected
from understanding the lives of the poor,
let us believe the words of Jesus:
I have seen Satan fall.

In a world where the demands of international debt
are more important than the health of children,
let us believe the words of Jesus:
I have seen Satan fall.

In a world where unjust laws and practices
privilege white people over others,
let us believe the words of Jesus:
I have seen Satan fall.

In a world where women are silenced and exploited
let us believe the words of Jesus:
I have seen Satan fall.

In a world where the lives of ordinary workers
are violated by the military,
let us believe the words of Jesus:
I have seen Satan fall.

In a world where the earth and its forests
are plundered and destroyed,
let us believe the words of Jesus:
I have seen Satan fall.

Janet Morley, England
Christian Aid
Luke 10:17-19

[13]

Leader:	We are wayfarers, following roads to the ends of the earth, pilgrims on our way to the end of the age.
All:	**"Behold, I am with you to the end of the age."**

Leader:	We are travellers on the road to freedom, a community of grace with good news for all we meet.
All:	**"Behold, I am with you to the end of the age."**

Leader:	We'll travel lightly, travel together, learn as we go; we are disciples, our mission is love, the journey is long.
All:	**"Behold, I am with you to the end of the age."**

Leader:	We travel with authority, fearful of none; we are sent, opponents of evil, heralds of hope.
All:	**"Behold, I am with you to the end of the age."**

Leader:	We'll travel with humility, no task is too small; we are servants, the cross is our compass, love is our sign.
All:	**"Behold, I am with you to the end of the age."**

Leader:	When the way is uncertain,
	shadows are sinister,
	and dangers threaten,
	we'll not be afraid, but take heart.
All:	**"Behold, I am with you**
	to the end of the age.

Campaign Kit, Philippines
Peace, Justice and Integrity of Creation,
Centre for Mindinao Studies, December, 1986
Matthew 10; Luke 10:1-2

[14]

The desert waits,
ready for those who come,
who come obedient to the Spirit's leading;
or who are driven,
because they will not come any other way.

The desert waits,
ready to let us know who we are—
the place of self-discovery.

And while we fear, and rightly,
the loneliness and emptiness and harshness,
we forget the angels,
whom we cannot see for our blindness,
but who come when God decides
that we need their help;
when we are ready
for what they can give us.

Ruth Burgess, England, 1989
Mark 1:12

[15]

Come, Lord,
do not smile and say you are already with us.
Millions do not know you,
and to us who do,
what is the difference?
What is the point of your presence
if our lives do not alter?
Change our lives,
shatter our complacency.
Make your word our life's purpose.
Take away the quietness of a clear conscience.
Press us uncomfortably.
For only thus
that other peace is made,
your peace.

Dom Helder Camara, Brazil
Matthew 10:34-39; Mark 10:17-22;
John 14:27, 20:19-23; James 2:14-17

[16]

God of vision,
we long to see your face
and are afraid to see it;
we long to break the grip of suffering,
and we cannot cast it out.
Uncover our faces
and expose us to your glory,
that we may comprehend the poor
in their suffering and insight,
and the world may be transfigured in you.
Amen.

Janet Morley, England
Christian Aid
Mark 9:1-29

[17]

My God, I need to have signs of your grace.
Give me your sacraments,
the first fruits of your Kingdom.

I thirst for smiles,
          for sweet odors,
          for soft words,
          for firm gestures,
          for truth and goodness,
          and for triumphs
          (no matter how small)
          of justice.

You know, O God, how hard it is to survive captivity
without any hope of the Holy City.
Sing to us, God, the songs of the promised land.
Serve us your manna in the desert.

Let there be, in some place,
a community of men, women, elderly, children, and new-
     born babies
  as a first fruit,
  as our appetizer,
  and our embrace of the future.
Amen.

Rubem A. Alves, Brazil
World YWCA/YMCA, 1984
Isaiah 65:17-25

[18]

For our incapacity to feel the sufferings of others,
and our tendency to live comfortably with injustice,
God forgive us.

For the self-righteousness that denies guilt,
and the self-interest that strangles compassion,
God forgive us.

For those who live their lives in careless unconcern,
who cry "Peace, peace," when there is no peace,
We ask your mercy.

For our failings in community,
our lack of understanding,
We ask your mercy.

For our lack of forgiveness, openness, sensitivity,
God forgive us.

For the times we were too eager to be better than others,
when we are too rushed to care,
when we are too tired to bother,
when we don't really listen,
when we are too quick to act from motives other than
    love,
God forgive us.

> PACSA, Pietermaritzburg, South Africa
> Jeremiah 6:13-15, 8:11

[19]

Blessed are the poor . . .
not the penniless
but those whose heart is free.

Blessed are those who mourn . . .
not those who whimper
but those who raise their voices.

Blessed are the meek . . .
not the soft
but those who are patient and tolerant.

Blessed are those who hunger and thirst for justice . . .
not those who whine
but those who struggle.

Blessed are the merciful . . .
not those who forget
but those who forgive.

Blessed are the pure in heart . . .
not those who act like angels
but those whose life is transparent.

Blessed are the peacemakers . . .
not those who shun conflict
but those who face it squarely.

Blessed are those who are persecuted for justice . . .
not because they suffer
but because they love.

P. Jacob, Santiago, Chile
Taken from *Compartir*
Matthew 5:3-12

[20]

God, we praise you for your love in Christ,
challenging all our definitions,
overturning all our stereotypes.

Wondering, amazed, in Christ we see you:
  the ruler of the universe, washing dirty feet;
  the creator of heaven and earth, hungry, cold, and
    tired;
  the savior and healer, wounded with the pain of the
    world,
  the almighty Lord, found with the weak and vulnerable.

God, help us to be strong in the love and liberty of Christ
so that we can follow the same pattern of service:
  with the inner security that frees us
    from the drive to seek reward or recognition;
  with the confidence to give those whom we serve
    the dignity of voicing their own needs;
  with the patience that does not try to impose your will
    or our own,
  but works and waits for your justice.

In the name of Christ.
Amen.

Jan Berry, England, 1990
Isaiah 53; Luke 9:58; John 13:1-20

[21]

Spirit of truth and judgment,
who alone can exorcise
the powers that grip our world,
at the point of crisis
give us your discernment,
that we may accurately name what is evil,
and know the way that leads to peace,
through Jesus Christ.
Amen.

Janet Morley, England
All Desires Known, London, 1988
Ephesians 6:12

[22]

God, our promised land;
Christ, our way,
our journey has become long and hard
because we wander about like nomads
not knowing where to go.
We are strangers in our own land,
without bread, a roof, a future.
But you came to find us
with your life-giving breath.
You, who are also displaced,
have become an exile with us.
You offer us anew the promised land.
Your spirit urges us toward
that joyous homecoming.

Displaced campesinos, Lima, Peru
Psalms for Life and Peace,
Latinamerica Press, November 5, 1987
Psalm 107; Matthew 2:13-18, 8:20

[23]

You asked for my hands
that you might use them for your purpose.
I gave them for a moment, then withdrew them
for the work was hard.

You asked for my mouth
to speak out against injustice.
I gave you a whisper that I might not be accused.

You asked for my eyes
to see the pain of poverty.
I closed them for I did not want to see.

You asked for my life
that you might work through me.
I gave a small part that I might not get too involved.

Lord, forgive my calculated efforts to serve you
only when it is convenient for me to do so,
only in those places where it is safe to do so,
and only with those who make it easy to do so.

Lord, forgive me,
renew me,
send me out
as a usable instrument
that I might take seriously
the meaning of your cross.

Joe Seremane, South Africa
Lifelines, Christian Aid
Proverbs 31:8-9; Mark 9:34-37

[24]

Lord, you placed me in the world
to be its salt.
I was afraid of committing myself,
afraid of being stained by the world.
I did not want to hear what "they" might say.
And my salt dissolved as if in water.
Forgive me, Jesus.

Lord, you placed me in the world
to be its light.
I was afraid of the shadows,
afraid of the poverty.
I did not want to know other people.
And my light slowly faded away.
Forgive me, Jesus.

Lord, you placed me in the world
to live in community.
Thus you taught me to love,
to share in life,
to struggle for bread and for justice,
your truth incarnate in my life.
So be it, Jesus.

Peggy M. de Cuehlo, Uruguay
Your Will Be Done,
Christian Conference of Asia Youth, 1984
Matthew 5:13-14

[25]

Jesus invites us to a way of celebration,
meeting and feasting with the humble and poor.
Let us walk his way with joy.

Jesus beckons us to a way of risk,
letting go of our security.
Let us walk his way with joy.

Jesus challenges us to listen to the voices
of those who have nothing to lose.
Let us walk his way with joy.

Jesus points us to a way of self-giving,
where power and status are overturned.
Let us walk his way with joy.

Jesus calls us to follow the way of the cross,
where despair is transformed by the promise of new life.
Let us walk his way with joy.

Jan Berry, England, 1990
Mark 9:34-37, 10:17-31, 12:41-44;
Luke 14:12-14, 22:24-27

HOLY WEEK

At the heart of the Christian faith is the memory of suffering. Holy Week is when we consciously call to mind and prayerfully live through the last days of Jesus' life: his facing of conflict, his betrayal and denial by friends, his unjust trial, and his death by torture. We believe that to participate in that memory is to place ourselves within the scope of salvation, because in that body on the cross God has "named all the violence of the world" (p. 94)—including our own— from which we long to be freed.

So it is the time when we corporately bring ourselves to remember what is unbearable, because without such memory we shall never be free. We would prefer not to remember. Particularly, we would prefer not to know how the memory preserved by our faith is shown forth today in hunger and blood across the world in the lives of the poor: in the overt violence of military repression, in the quiet and seemly violence of international debt, and in the seizure and violation of the land on which the poor depend. But salvation for all requires such memory.

The story of the Last Supper, significantly, gives us something to *do* in memory of Christ—namely, to eat and drink what are both the tokens of his death and the means of nourishment and life. The bodily, mundane elements of a meal can recall for us the labor and the suffering of the poor, and also their celebration. The workers in a community soup kitchen speak of Christ as literally "the food of the poor"—"a warm loaf that makes us a family." It is true that the celebration of the Last Supper very quickly became associated with the exclusion and humiliation of the poor (1 Corinthians 11); and we need to be warned of the danger of eating and drinking without discerning the broken body of our whole human community. As a Filipino bishop has remarked, if we celebrate the eucharist without that awareness, "we embarrass the poor outrageously."

On Good Friday, following the events of the Passion narrative, some ancient traditions of the church have used the "reproaches" — a litany in which God speaks a poignant and questioning lament. The acts of salvation performed by God throughout history are contrasted, with piercing irony, with the unspeakable treatment meted out to the savior himself. In one of the prayers that follows, the old form is kept but the contrasting reference is to our treatment of each other and the earth (pp. 89-91).

The cross itself speaks of helplessness and silence. Among those who know what it is to be silenced or to be unheard, this silence on the part of God is a profound point of identification. Elsa Tamez of Mexico writes:

> God remains silent so that men and women may speak, protest and struggle . . . When God is silent and men and women cry, God cries in solidarity with them, but God doesn't intervene. God waits for the shouts of protest. Then the Almighty begins to speak again, but in dialogue with us. ("Letter to Job," *New Eyes for Reading*, World Council of Churches, 1986)

The silence of the crucified is "God's word" (p. 93) — God who "suffers with the world not safe above" (p. 100).

And so we bring to the foot of the cross not only our own sins but the evil and violence of the world — everything within our history and our present of which we are most ashamed and frightened; the sheer intransigence of poverty and the violent, self-interested arrangements that enforce it; our sense of helplessness to change. And we offer ourselves to a God who shares our pain and failure, that "what is sown in dishonor may be raised in glory, and what is sown in weakness may be raised in power" (p. 87).

HOLY THURSDAY

[1]

Lord Jesus Christ,
because you broke bread with the poor,
you were looked on with contempt.

Because you broke bread with the sinful and outcast,
you were looked on as ungodly.

Because you broke bread with the joyful,
you were called a winebiber and a glutton.

Because you broke bread in the upstairs room,
you sealed your acceptance of the way of the cross.

Because you broke bread on the road to Emmaus,
you made scales fall from the disciples' eyes.

**Because you broke bread and shared it,
we will do so, too,
and ask your blessing.**

> "Your Will Be Done," San Antonio Conference
> on "Mission in Christ's Way," 1990
> Luke 15:1-10, 23:14-27, 24:13-35; Matthew 11:16-19

[2]

We know that we come together for the Lord's supper
   in a world where one is hungry and another is drunk;
   where we ourselves are well-fed, secure, and articulate;
   where success and wealth are worshiped, and the cross
       of Christ is a folly and a scandal;
   where there are divisions we recognize and those we
       still fail to see.

Let us wait for one another before we eat and drink,
   and bring these divisions with us;
let us wait for the hungry and the dispossessed,
   remembering those we have met, and in whom we
       have seen the face of God;
let us wait for those who, in their struggle for justice,
   have challenged us and changed us;
let us wait for those who, with nothing to give,
   have greeted us as guests and shown us the generosity
       of God;
let us wait for those whom we oppose,
   who actively undermine the poor,
   or in their apathy support injustice.

Let us bring to this table those with whom we long to
       share,
   and those we disapprove of;
   and in our dividedness,
let us proclaim the Lord's death until he comes.

Janet Morley, England
Christian Aid
1 Corinthians 11:17-29

[3]

Lord God,
in Jesus, you came in the body:
flesh of our flesh, bone of our bone.
We thank you that you did not remain an idea,
even a religious idea,
but walked, wept, and washed feet among us.
By your love,
change our ideas, especially our religious ideas,
into living signs of your work and will.

**Through our lives and by our prayers,
your kingdom come.**

Lord God,
in Jesus your body was broken
by the cowardly and the powerful.
The judgment hall of Pilate
knew your silence as surely
as your critics knew your voice.
In word and silence,
take on the powerful of the world today:
those whose words sentence some to cruelty
or unmerited redundancy;
those whose word transfers wealth or weapons
for the sake of profit or prejudice;
those whose silence condones the injustice
they have the power to change.

O Savior of the poor, liberate your people.

**Through our lives and by our prayers,
your kingdom come.**

Wild Goose Worship Group, *A Wee Worship Book*, 1989
Mark 15:1-5; John 1:14

We take bread
symbol of labor, exploited, degraded,
symbol of life.
We will break the bread
because Christ, the source of life,
was broken for the exploited and downtrodden.

We take wine
symbol of blood, spilled in war and conflict,
symbol of new life.
We will drink the wine
because Christ, the peace of the world,
was killed by violence.

Now bread and wine are before us,
the memory of our meals,
our working, our talking;
the story which shapes us,
the grieving and the pain,
the oppressor who lies deep in our own soul;
the seeking and the loving.

And we give thanks
for all that holds us together in our humanity;
that binds us to all who live and have lived,
who have cried and are crying,
who hunger and are thirsty,
who pine for justice,
and who hold out for the time that is coming.

And in this we are bound to Jesus,
who, in the same night that he was betrayed,
took bread and gave you thanks;
he broke it and gave it to his disciples, saying:

"Take, eat; this is my body which is given for you;
do this in remembrance of me."
In the same way after supper
he took the cup and gave you thanks;
he gave it to them saying:
"Drink this, all of you;
this is my blood of the new covenant,
which is shed for you and for many
for the forgiveness of sins.
Do this as often as you drink it
in remembrance of me."

This is the death we celebrate.
This is the new life we proclaim.
This is the vision we await.

"Eucharist of Liberation" used in a London house church
Living Beyond Our Means,
World Student Christian Federation, 1985
Luke 22:14-23

[5]

God, food of the poor;
Christ, our bread,
give us a taste of the tender bread
from your creation's table;
bread newly taken from your heart's oven,
food that comforts and nourishes us.
A loaf of community that makes us human,
joined hand in hand, working and sharing.
A warm loaf that makes us a family;
sacrament of your body,
your wounded people.

Workers in community soup kitchens in Lima
Psalms for Life and Peace, Latinamerica Press, 1987
John 6:48-58

GOOD FRIDAY

[6] EUCHARISTIC PRAYER FOR GOOD FRIDAY

O holy Wisdom of our God,
eternally offensive to our wisdom,
and compassionate toward our weakness,
we praise you and give you thanks,
because you emptied yourself of power
and entered our struggle,
taking upon yourself our unprotected flesh.
You opened wide your arms for us upon the cross,
becoming scandal for our sake,
that you might sanctify even the grave
to be a bed of hope to your people.

Therefore, with those who are detained without justice,
     abandoned or betrayed by friends,
whose bodies are violated or in pain;
with those who have died alone
without dignity, comfort, or hope;
and with all the company of saints
who have carried you in their wounds
that they may be bodied forth with life,
we praise you, saying:

Holy, holy, holy,
vulnerable God.
Heaven and earth are full of your glory;
hosanna in the highest.
Blessed is the one
who comes in the name of God;
hosanna in the highest.

Blessed is our brother Jesus,
bone of our bone and flesh of our flesh,

from whom the cup of suffering did not pass;
who, on the night that he was betrayed,
took bread, gave thanks, broke it, and said:
"This is my body, which is for you.
Do this to remember me."
In the same way also the cup, after supper, saying:
"This cup is the new covenant in my blood.
Do this, whenever you drink it,
to remember me."

Christ has died.
Christ is risen.
Christ will come again.

Therefore, as we eat this bread and drink this cup,
we are proclaiming Christ's death until he comes.
In the body broken and the blood poured out,
we restore to memory and hope
the broken and unremembered victims
of tyranny and sin;
and we long for the bread of tomorrow,
and the wine of the age to come.
Come then, life-giving spirit of our God,
brood over these bodily things,
and make us one body with Christ,
that we, who are baptized into his death,
may walk in newness of life;
that what is sown in dishonor
may be raised in glory,
and what is sown in weakness
may be raised in power.

Janet Morley, England
Christian Aid
Genesis 2:23; Matthew 6:11; 1 Corinthians 1:23, 15:42-43;
2 Corinthians 5:21; Philippians 2:1-11

[7]

God, freedom for the oppressed;
Christ, our liberator,
from deep within our prisons
we cry to you; hear our lament.
Take note of our protest,
for we are held captive.
Break the circle of death
that keeps us wounded.
Come down to the blackness of this hell,
we are alone, gagged, hungry.
But despite the chains of this captivity,
life still throbs
and we keep on living.

Those who work with prisoners in Lima, Peru
Psalms for Life and Peace, Latinamerica Press, 1987
Psalm 88

[8]

Bless your people, Lord,
who have walked too long in this night of pain.
For the child has no more tears to cry
and the old people no song of joy to sing,
and the blood of our youth drains away in the gutters.
The cry from the cross is heard throughout the land.
The pain in your nailed hands is carried by the worker.
Terrible thirst is in the mouth of the farmer,
too many women mourn the loss of their sons,
and all the earth is turned into another Calvary.
With your spirit, Lord, we cry for peace.
With your spirit, we struggle to be free.

National Council of Churches of the Philippines,
14th Biennial Convention Resource Book, 1989
Isaiah 9:2; John 19:23-30

[9]

Holy God,
holy and strange,
holy and intimate,
have mercy on us.

O my people, what have I done to you?
How have I offended you?
Answer me.

I brooded over the abyss,
with my words I called forth creation:
but you have brooded on destruction,
and manufactured the means of chaos.

O my people, what have I done to you?
How have I offended you?
Answer me.

I breathed life into your bodies,
and carried you tenderly in my arms:
but you have armed yourselves for war,
breathing out threats of violence.

O my people, what have I done to you?
How have I offended you?
Answer me.

I made the desert blossom before you,
I fed you with an open hand:
but you have grasped the children's food,
and laid waste fertile lands.

O my people, what have I done to you?
How have I offended you?
Answer me.

I abandoned my power like a garment,
choosing your unprotected flesh:
but you have robed yourselves in privilege,
and chosen to despise the abandoned.

O my people, what have I done to you?
How have I offended you?
Answer me.

Holy God,
holy and strange,
holy and intimate,
have mercy on us.

I would have gathered you to me as a lover,
and shown you the ways of peace:
but you have desired security,
and you would not surrender your self.

O my people, what have I done to you?
How have I offended you?
Answer me.

I have torn the veil of my glory,
transfiguring the earth:
but you have disfigured my beauty,
and turned away your face.

O my people, what have I done to you?
How have I offended you?
Answer me.

I have labored to deliver you,
as a woman delights to give life:
but you have delighted in bloodshed,
and labored to bereave the world.

O my people, what have I done to you?
How have I offended you?
Answer me.

I have followed you with the power of my spirit,
to seek truth and heal the oppressed:
but you have been following a lie,
and returned to your own comfort.

O my people, what have I done to you?
How have I offended you?
Answer me.

Holy God,
holy and strange,
holy and intimate,
have mercy on us.

Janet Morley, England, 1988
Genesis 1, 2:7; Psalm 22:9-10, 104:28;
Isaiah 35:1, 46:3-4, 53:1-4; Matthew 27:51;
Luke 13:34, 19:41-44; John 16:20-22

[10]

Hands like these
    Were hammered on the tree.
Feet like our feet
    Were pierced.
A head like our head
    Bore the shameful thorns.

Gwenallt, 1959
Gwreiddiau, Gwasg Gomer
Welsh Pilgrim's Manual, ed. Brendan O'Malley, Gomer, 1989

[11]

"Daughters of Jerusalem, do not weep for me, but weep for yourselves and for your children." (Luke 23:28)

Jesus,
You have heard our tears:
the tears women have shed in silence
   because we were afraid to be heard;
the tears women have held back
   thinking we deserved violence;
the tears we have not held back
   but were not comforted;
the tears women have wept alone
   because we would not ask to be held;
the tears women weep together
   because our sisters cannot feed their children;
   because our sisters live in fear;
   because the earth herself is threatened.

So we weep.

> Janet Morley, England
> Christian Aid

[12]

O Lord Jesus,
stretch forth your wounded hands in blessing over your
   people,
to heal and to restore,
and to draw them to yourself and to one another in love.
   Amen.

> Prayer from the Middle East
> *With All God's People*, World Council of Churches, 1989

[13]

With his hands
nailed wide before us
how he weeps, then laughs
in the pain
of a simple "No"
issuing forth from heaven:
leaving him
without a land
leaving him
without a home
leaving him
without a mother
leaving him
leaving him . . .

Eulalia Bernard, Costa Rica
Lovers and Comrades, ed. Amanda Hopkinson,
Women's Press, 1989
Mark 15:33-37

[14]

In the pain, misfortune, oppression,
and death of the people,
God is silent.
God is silent on the cross,
in the crucified.
And this silence is God's word,
God's cry.
In solidarity,
God speaks the language of love.

Jon Sobrino, El Salvador
With All God's People, World Council of Churches, 1989
Philippians 2:5-8

[15]

O Christ,
in whose body was named
all the violence of the world,
and in whose memory is contained
our profoundest grief,

we lay open to you:
the violence done to us in time before memory;
the unremembered wounds that have misshaped our
    lives;
the injuries we cannot forget
and have not forgiven.

The remembrance of them is grievous to us;
the burden of them is intolerable.

We lay open to you:
the violence done in our name in time before memory;
the unremembered wounds we have inflicted;
the injuries we cannot forget
and for which we have not been forgiven.

The remembrance of them is grievous to us;
the burden of them is intolerable.

We lay open to you:
those who have pursued a violent knowledge the world
    cannot forget;
those caught up in violence they have refused to name;
those who have enacted violence which they have not
    repented.

The remembrance of them is grievous to us;
the burden of them is intolerable.

We lay open to you:
the victims of violence whose only memorial is our anger;
those whose suffering was sustained on our behalf;
those whose continued oppression provides the ground
     we stand on.

The remembrance of them is grievous to us;
the burden of them is intolerable.

Hear what comfortable words our savior Christ says to all
     who truly turn to God:

Come to me, all you who labor and are heavy-laden,
and I will give you rest.
Take my yoke upon you, and learn of me,
for I am gentle and lowly in heart,
and you will find rest for your souls.
For my yoke is easy, and my burden light.

We wholeheartedly repent
of the evil we have done,
and of the evil done on our behalf;
and we look for grace to offer forgiveness,
and to know ourselves forgiven.

Janet Morley, England, 1988

[16]

I believe, although everything hides you from my faith.
I believe, although everything shouts No! to me.
I believe, although everything may seem to die.
I believe, although I no longer would wish to live,
  because I have founded my life
  on a sincere word,
  on the word of a Friend,
  on the word of God.
I believe, although I feel alone in pain.
I believe, although I see people hating.
I believe, although I see children weep,
  because I have learned with certainty
  that you come to meet us in the hardest hours,
  with your love and your light.
I believe, but increase my faith.

Livro de Cantos, Porte Alegre, Brazil, 1977
All Year Round, British Council of Churches, 1987
Job 23; Psalm 77; Jeremiah 15:15-21; Mark 9:24

[17]

The cross is the way of the lost
the cross is the staff of the lame
the cross is the guide of the blind
the cross is the strength of the weak
the cross is the hope of the hopeless
the cross is the freedom of the slaves
the cross is the water of the seeds
the cross is the consolation of the bonded laborers
the cross is the source of those who seek water
the cross is the cloth of the naked.

A 10th century African hymn
With All God's People, World Council of Churches, 1989
1 Corinthians 1:18-30

[18]

To you, O Lord,
on bended knees
our heads we bow in prayer:
that you may hear
our cry for blood-drenched lands
and their exhausted people,
who have seen too much death,
and have been afraid too long
to understand your love,
comprehend your presence,
acknowledge your goodness
and concern for them, a battered people;
yearning for freedom
as they bear your cross.
Amen.

Lesley G. Anderson
Panama/United Kingdom, 1989

[19]

Merciful God,
we meet each other today at this cross
as inhabitants of one world.
As those who inflict wounds on each other:
be merciful to us.
As those who deny justice to others:
be merciful to us.
As those who seize wealth:
be merciful to us.
As those who put others on trial:
be merciful to us.
As those who refuse to receive:
be merciful to us.

As those afraid of this world's torment:
be merciful to us.

Giver of life,
we wait with you
to bear your hope to earth's darkest places.
Where love is denied:
let love break through.
Where justice is destroyed:
let righteousness rule.
Where hope is crucified:
let faith persist.
Where peace is no more:
let passion live on.
Where truth is denied
let the struggle continue.

Silence

Reach into this silent darkness
with your love;
deepen the terror of this moment
into new hope;
relieve the hideous cries
with your quiet voice of peace;
that here we may know
your salvation,
your glory,
your future
in Jesus Christ, the crucified Lord. Amen.

Robin Green, England
Let All the World, ed. Wendy Robins, USPG, 1990
Mark 15:53-72

HOLY SATURDAY

[20]

Nailed to a cross because you would not
compromise on your convictions.
Nailed to a cross because you would not
bow down before insolent might.
My Savior, you were laughed at,
derided, bullied, spat upon,
but with unbroken spirit,
Liberator God, you died.

Many young lives are sacrificed
because they will not bend;
many young people are in prison
for following your lead.
Daily, you are crucified,
my Savior, you are sacrificed
in prison cells and torture rooms
of cruel and ruthless powers.

The promise of resurrection,
the power of hope it holds,
and the vision of a just new order,
you proclaimed that first Easter morning.
Therefore, dear Savior, we can affirm
that although bodies are mutilated and broken,
the spirit refuses submission.
Your voice will never be silenced,
Great Liberating God.

Aruna Gnanadason, India
Your Will Be Done, Christian Conference of Asia Youth, 1984
Matthew 10:28

[21]

The cross points us to God,
  its purpose clear:
 the one who gave us life
   still holds us dear.
God suffers with the world,
  not safe above:
 word rooted to the earth
   as pledge of love.
Dark shadow of our fears,
  our badge of shame,
 it bears the one we killed
   to take our blame.
His arms reach out to grasp
  all humankind;
 he welcomes all who come
   to seek and find.
The violence of years
  is shaped in wood,
 yet here a healing tree
   turns all to good.
The cross stands empty now:
  an end to strife;
 we praise the God who plants
   the tree of life.

Christopher Ellis, England, 1990
Ephesians 2:13-16

[22]

Lord Jesus, by your cross and resurrection — **deliver us**
by your witness to the truth — **deliver us**
by your passion and death — **deliver us**

by your victory over the grave — **deliver us**
from the desire for power — **deliver us**
from the conspiracy of silence — **deliver us**
from the worship of weapons — **deliver us**
from the slaughter of the peoples — **deliver us**
from the nightmare of hunger — **deliver us**
from peace that is no peace — **deliver us**
from security that is no security — **deliver us**
from the politics of terror — **deliver us**
from the plundering of the earth's resources — **deliver us**
from the dispossession of the poor — **deliver us**
from the despair of this age — **deliver us**

By the light of the gospel — **give us peace**
by the good news for the poor — **give us peace**
by your healing of our wounds — **give us peace**
by faith in your word — **give us peace**
by hunger and thirst for justice — **give us peace**
by the coming of the Kingdom — **give us peace**

Linda Frewin and Tony Bartlett, England
"Litany for Peace," *Prayers for Peacemakers*,
ed. Valerie Flessati, Kevin Mayhew Publishers, 1988
Isaiah 53

[23]

Lord: Help us to see in the groaning of creation
not death throes but birth pangs;
help us to see in suffering a promise for the future,
because it is a cry against the inhumanity of the present.
Help us to glimpse in protest the dawn of justice,
in the Cross the pathway to resurrection,
and in suffering the seeds of joy.

Rubem Alves, Brazil
All Year Round, British Council of Churches, 1987
Romans 8:18-25

EASTER

Easter, the announcement of the defeat of death by life, is strangely problematic for many of us in this culture to celebrate. Although (or perhaps because) most of us are surrounded with every protection from hunger, disease, and threat of death, we cannot quite believe this statement of triumph over despair. It may be no coincidence that the great majority of prayers in this section come from developing countries, although that was not particularly the balance that was sought. Although we inherit a deep and moving tradition of poetic reflection on the theme of resurrection, the references in our culture are profoundly personal. It is as if we lack a believable language for corporate, unqualified hope for the *world* — even if our faith should offer us this.

Perhaps one of the problems is that we expect Easter to provide an uncomplicated and uncostly sort of joy, and are puzzled when it does not. I take courage from the mood of the gospel resurrection narratives, which on close inspection have a good deal more to say about shock, fear, and a bemused lack of recognition than about immediate delight. It is clear that the first disciples, for all their good intentions, found it hard even to see, let alone understand, the earth-shaking change that this "good news" implies. It may be that as the relatively wealthy in this world we both hope for and fear the changes that the poorest long for and need. And so, to pray at Easter in solidarity with the poor may require us to start from an acknowledgment of our own fear and despair. We pray: "Although we fear change; although we are not ready; although we'd rather weep and run away: Roll back the stone" (p. 117).

By contrast, it is those who have literally endured the cost and the risk of Holy Week who are the readiest to hear the message of resurrection and claim it as their truth. We here, when speaking of the possibility of new life through death, are most likely to be speaking metaphorically. But among some of the churches of the poor has arisen a new affirmation of the ancient tradition of Christian martyrdom. Jon Sobrino, a Jesuit priest from El Salvador, in reflecting on the political assassination of all his community household startlingly calls it "good news." He deems it so because, along with countless other killings, it declares that in that place the church is truly sharing the dangers and sufferings of the poor. So the new "creeds" emerging from committed and vibrant churches in Central and Latin America often speak of "the blood of our martyrs" (p. 107), meaning real modern blood and not stained glass; and they understand it to be the lifeblood of a church that preaches resurrection.

So it is this Easter section that points up most vividly the distance that lies between those who have or who have not, as individuals or communities, explicitly confronted the powers of evil, and moved beyond the fear of death to a place of inexplicable freedom and life: "I am no longer afraid of death . . ." (p. 120).

But whether or not we can understand such freedom, we can pray for the capacity to recognize it and choose the path that leads to it. And we can celebrate that disturbing resurrection peace given by Jesus, which resembles not "the silence of cemeteries" (Romero) or the quietude produced by hunger, repression, or self-satisfaction, but is "the babble of tongues set free, the thunder of dancing feet" (p. 119).

[1]

It is the Lord, in the dawning,
                in the renewal,
                in the arrival,
                in the new day.

It is the Lord, in the crowd,
                in the church,
                in the conversation,
                in the crisis.

It is the Lord, in our joys,
                in our sorrows,
                in our sickness,
                in our health.

It is the Lord, in the stable,
                in the humble,
                in the stranger,
                in the poor.

It is the Lord, risen and returned,
                alive for evermore,
                giving me new life,
                saving me in strife,
                    It is the Lord.

David Adam, England
Times and Seasons, Triangle, 1989
John 20:1-18

[2]

When the hour comes,
you shall change my desert into a waterfall,
you shall anoint my head with fresh oil
and your strength shall overcome my weakness.

You shall guide my feet into your footsteps
and I will walk the narrow path
that leads to your house.

You shall tell me when and where
I will walk your path totally bathed in joy.
In the meantime,
I ask you, Lord, you who awaken
in the most intimate place in my soul
the Feast of Life!
That of the Empty Tomb!
That of the Victorious Cross!

Let your voice mistaken as the Gardener's
awaken my hearing every morning
with news that's always fresh:
"Go and tell my brothers and sisters
that I have overcome death,
that there is a place for everyone
there where the New Nation is built.

There, where neither earth, love, or joy
can be bought or sold,
where wine and milk
are shared without money and without price."

Julia Esquivel, Guatemala
Threatened with Resurrection,
The Brethren Press, United States, 1982
Isaiah 55:1-2; John 20

[3]

Firmly I believe, Lord,
that your prodigious mind
created this whole earth.
To your artist's hand beauty owed its birth:
the stars and the moon,
the cottages, the lakes,
little boats bobbing down river to the sea,
vast coffee plantations,
white cotton fields
and the forests felled by the criminal axe.

In you I believe,
maker of thought and music,
maker of the wind,
maker of peace and love.

Christ the worker, I believe you,
light of light and God's true
only begotten son,
that to save the world you
in Mary's humble womb grew
and became human.
I believe that you were beaten,
treated with scorn,
martyred on the cross
under Pilate's command.

I believe in you, friend,
human Christ, Christ the worker,
death you've overcome.
Your fearful suffering brought
the new human being
born for freedom.
You still rise again

each time we raise an arm
to defend the people
from profiteering dominion,
because you're alive on the farm,
in the factory, and in school.
I believe your fight goes on,
I believe in your Resurrection.

"Creed" from the Nicaraguan Mass

[4]

We believe in God, creator of the earth,
creator of life and freedom,
hope of the poor.

We believe in Jesus Christ,
friend in suffering,
companion in the resurrection,
way of peace.

We believe in the Spirit,
that holy force impelling the poor
to build a church of the beatitudes.

We recognize one baptism
in the blood of our martyrs;
we confess our faith in the law of love.
We wait for the resurrection of the people,
and joyfully praise our Lord,
who has looked upon the disinherited,
those who have no bread,
no home, and no land.

Fray Guillermo Chavez, Ecuador
"Iglesia Solidaria," Latinamerica Press,
September 3, 1987

[5]

When we stand gazing upwards, bring us down to earth:
    with the love of a friend
    through the songs of the sorrowing
    in the faces of the hungry.

When we look to you for action, demand some work from
    us:
    by your touch of fire
    your glance of reproof
    your fearful longing.

As ruler over all:
    love us into action
    fire us with your zeal
    enrich us with your grace
    to make us willing subjects of your rule.

Janet Nightingale, England
Christian Aid
Acts 1 and 2

[6]

Risen Jesus,
we thank you for your greeting,
"Peace be with you."
The *shalom* of God,
deep lasting peace;
peace that brings inner calm;
that keeps a person steady in the storm;
that faces the persecutor without fear
and proclaims the good news
with courage and with joy.
This is the peace that reconciles
sister to brother, black to white,

rich and poor, young and old,
but not a peace that is quiet
in the face of oppression and injustice.
This is peace with God,
the peace that passes understanding.

John Johansen-Berg
Prayers of the Way, Community for Reconciliation, 1990
John 20:19-29; Philippians 4:7

[7]

God of power,
God of people,
You are the life of all
that lives,
energy
that fills the earth,
vitality
that brings to birth,
the impetus
toward making whole
whatever is bruised
or broken.
In You we grow
to know the truth
that sets all creation free.
You are the song
the whole earth sings,
the promise
liberation brings,
now and forever.

Miriam Therese Winter, United States
WomanPrayer, WomanSong: Resources for Ritual,
Meyer Stone, 1987
Psalm 104

[8]

Above any government and sovereignty,
above the riot police and the tanks,
above vested interests and corruption,
above political establishments,
above all things—the reign of Christ.

Lord, we were going to do something about poverty,
about hunger, ignorance, and disease,
but it was all too much for us,
beyond our giving and our understanding.

Lord, we were going to do something about violence,
about the arms race, nuclear weapons,
and those who make a profit out of war,
but we couldn't make sense of it,
and we couldn't see what we should do.

Lord, we were going to do something about ecology,
about the disappearance of the forests,
the rare species and irreplaceable plants;
but it really is very difficult,
and none of us is expert in these matters.

Lord, we are good at learning a little,
and wringing our hands in helplessness.
May we take the power you have given,
and set about claiming our inheritance.

> Stephen Orchard, England
> "He has put all things under his feet,"
> *All the Glorious Names*,
> United Reformed Church Prayer Handbook, 1989
> Philippians 2:9-11

[9]

O Lord our God,
we thank you for the many people throughout the ages
who have followed your way of life joyfully:
for the many saints and martyrs, men and women,
who have offered up their very lives,
so that your life abundant may become manifest.
**For your love and faithfulness we will at all times
praise you.**

O Lord, we thank you for those who chose the way of
Jesus Christ.
In the midst of trial, they held out hope;
in the midst of hatred, they kindled love;
in the midst of persecutions, they witnessed to your
power;
in the midst of despair, they clung to your promise.
**For your love and faithfulness we will at all times
praise you.**

O Lord, we thank you for the truth they passed on to us:
that it is by giving that we shall receive;
it is by becoming weak that we shall be strong;
it is by loving others that we shall be loved;
it is by offering ourselves that the kingdom will unfold;
it is by dying that we shall inherit life everlasting.
Lord, give us courage to follow your way of life.
**For your love and faithfulness we will at all times
praise you.**

National Council of Churches of the Philippines,
14th Biennial Convention Resource Book, 1989
Matthew 10:16-42

[10]

Stay with us, Lord,
for the day is far spent
and we have not yet recognized your face
in each of our brothers and sisters.

Stay with us, Lord,
for the day is far spent
and we have not yet shared your bread
in grace with our brothers and sisters.

Stay with us, Lord,
for the day is far spent
and we have not listened to your Word
in the words of our brothers and sisters.

Stay with us, Lord,
because our very night becomes day
when you are there.

"Who Do You Say That I Am?", Seoul, 1989
Worship Book of the World Alliance of Reformed Churches
Luke 24:1-35

[11]

Alleluia
Speak, Jesus, Word of God.
It's your turn to speak. Alleluia.
Alleluia
Brother, who speaks truth to his brothers and sisters, give
     us your new freedom.
Free from profit and from fear,
we will live in gospel;
we will shout in gospel: Alleluia.
Alleluia

No power will silence us. Alleluia.
Alleluia
Against the orders of hate
you bring us the law of love.
In the face of so many lies
you are the truth out loud.
Amid so much news of death
you have the word of life.
After so many false promises, frustrated hopes,
you have, Lord Jesus, the last word,
and we have put all our trust in you. Alleluia.
Alleluia
Your truth will set us free. Alleluia.
Alleluia.

Pedro Casaldáliga, Brazil
Misa dos Quilombos, trans. Tony Graham, Christian Aid

[12]

I believe that behind the mist the sun waits.
I believe that beyond the dark night it is raining stars.
I believe in secret volcanoes and the world below.
I believe that this lost ship will reach port.
They will not rob me of hope, it shall not be broken.
My voice is filled to overflowing
with the desire to sing, the desire to sing.
I believe in reason, and not in the force of arms;
I believe that peace will be sown throughout the earth.
I believe in our nobility, created in the image of God,
and with free will reaching for the skies.
They will not rob me of hope, it shall not be broken,
it shall not be broken.

Chile
Confessing Our Faith Around the World IV, South America,
World Council of Churches, 1985

[13]

We are the children of the sun are we,
who write in the shadows of evening,
who walk in the dark of the night,
who arise in the light of the dawn,
who go barefoot in the womb of the world,
who sow the field,
who grow the daily bread,
who know the language of the wind,
who see the rain fall on a parched land
and on tired faces,
who plough the furrows of the old,
who bring the bones to bloom,
who consecrate bread in our own flesh,
who break chains and discover the way.

Michele Najlis, Nicaragua
Lovers and Comrades, ed. Amanda Hopkinson,
Women's Press, 1989

[14]

Soft the Master's love song,
and beautiful to hear:
"Come to me, you poor,
all who stumble in distress;
release from toil I offer,
come to me for rest."

"If you're burdened down,
let me bear the strain for you.
You must not despair:
through my Easter death has died;
so journey on with courage,
I am by your side."

Jesus, you are strong,
I am weak, a foolish child;
I will turn to you,
boast in you alone, my friend.
Your words give life to live by,
love that has no end.

Rudolf Pantou, Indonesia
Sound the Bamboo, Asian Institute for Liturgy
and Music, 1990
Matthew 11:28-30

[15]

Oh people, you shall not drown in your tears
But tears shall bathe your wounds.

Oh people, you shall not die from hunger
But hunger shall feed your souls.

Oh people, you are not weak in your suffering
But strong and brave with knowing.

Oh people, if you have known struggle
Only then are you capable of loving.

Oh people, be aware of the love you have

Let not your tears submerge it
Let not your hunger eat it
Let not your suffering destroy it—

Oh people, bitterness does not replace a grain of love:
Let us be awake in our love.

Noorie Cassim, South Africa
Cry Justice, John de Gruchy, Orbis Books, 1986
Isaiah 40:28-31, 43:1-7

[16]

Life goes beyond death,
because life is called to life, not death.
That is the plan of its creator.
But life blossoms into full flower
only in those who nurture life
here on this earth;
in those who defend its rights,
protect its dignity,
and are even willing to accept death
in their witness to it.
Those who violate life,
deprive others of life,
and crucify the living,
will remain seeds that fail to take root,
buds that fail to open,
and cocoons that are forever closed in upon themselves.
Their fate is absolute and total frustration.

All those who die like Jesus,
sacrificing their lives out of love
for the sake of a more dignified human life,
will inherit life in all its fullness.
They are like grains of wheat,
dying to produce life,
being buried in the ground
only to break through and grow.

Leonardo Boff, Brazil
Way of the Cross, Way of Justice, Orbis Books, 1980
John 12:24-25

[17]

When we are all despairing;
when the world is full of grief;
when we see no way ahead,
    and hope has gone away:

Roll back the stone.

Although we fear change;
although we are not ready;
although we'd rather weep
    and run away:

Roll back the stone.

Because we're coming with the women;
because we hope where hope is vain;
because you call us from the grave
    and show the way:

Roll back the stone.

Janet Morley, England
Christian Aid
Mark 16:1-8

[18]

Goodness is stronger than evil;
love is stronger than hate;
light is stronger than darkness;
life is stronger than death;
victory is ours through Jesus who loved us.

Desmond Tutu, South Africa
John 1:5

[19]

In the face of the struggle for freedom,
Give us strength.
In the face of decisions about freedom,
Give us wisdom.
In the practice of freedom,
Give us guidance.
From the dangers of freedom,
Give us protection.
In the life of freedom,
Give us joy.
In the way in which we use our freedom,
Give us a clear vision.

South American Council of Churches
"A Litany for Human Rights," *All Year Round*,
British Council of Churches, 1988

[20]

When the day comes on which our victory
    will shine like a torch in the night,
    it will be like a dream.
We will laugh and sing for joy.
Then the other nations will say about us,
    "The Lord did great things for them."
Indeed, he is doing great things for us;
that is why we are happy in our suffering.

Lord, break the chains of humiliation and death,
    just as on that glorious morning
    when you were raised.
Let those who weep as they sow the seeds of justice and
        freedom
gather the harvest of peace and reconciliation.

Those who weep as they go out as instruments of your
     love
   will come back singing with joy,
   as they will witness the disappearance of hate
and the manifestation of your love in your world.

Zephania Kameeta, Namibia
"Psalm 26," *Why O Lord?* World Council of Churches, 1986

[21]

Say "no" to peace if what they mean by peace
   is the quiet misery of hunger,
      the frozen stillness of fear,
         the silence of broken spirits,
            the unborn hopes of the oppressed.

Tell them that peace is the shouting of children at play,
   the babble of tongues set free,
      the thunder of dancing feet,
         and a father's voice singing.

Say "no" to peace if what they mean by peace
   is a rampart of gleaming missiles,
      the arming of distant wars,
         money at ease in its castle
            and grateful poor at the gate.

Tell them that peace is the hauling down of flags,
   the forging of guns into ploughs,
      the giving of fields to the landless,
         and hunger a fading dream.

Brian Wren, England
Oxford University Press, 1986
Jeremiah 6:14; Micah 4:1-6; Luke 16:19-31

[22]

I am no longer afraid of death,
I know well
its dark and cold corridors
leading to life.

I am afraid rather of that life
which does not come out of death
which cramps our hands
and retards our march.

I am afraid of my fear
and even more of the fear of others,
who do not know where they are going,
who continue clinging
to what they consider to be life
which we know to be death!

I live each day to kill death;
I die each day to beget life,
and in this dying unto death,
I die a thousand times and
am reborn another thousand
through that love
from my people,
which nourishes hope!

Julia Esquivel, Guatemala
Threatened with Resurrection,
The Brethren Press, United States, 1982
John 12: 24-25; Romans 6:3-11

PENTECOST/ORDINARY TIME

At Pentecost, the church celebrates the coming of the Spirit—the outpouring of the sudden power of God to transform a wounded and disillusioned band of stragglers into a community that changed the world. It was a power that was both awaited in obedience, and utterly unexpected in its energy and urgency. It generated both a deep interior fire, and immediate, compelling, and outrageous public witness.

The prayers that follow pick up the wealth of traditional images associated with the power of the Spirit, and celebrate them in the struggles of today's world. God's power is potentially overwhelming, like the natural forces of wind, fire, storm, and flood. It is power to break down what is corrupt in the world's patterns of thought and dominance. But the Spirit is also seen as the "breath of love," the giver of life, the remaker of community, the "waker of the oppressed" (p. 138), the one who sings in the hearts of the poor (p. 123). Above all, the prayers reflect the power of the Spirit to integrate profound change of heart with exuberant and effective action within the world. It is not enough (though it is necessary!) to be set on fire personally with the love of God. We have to recognize, with Bishop Pedro Casaldáliga of Brazil, that "solidarity is love made public."

How then do we pray for and in the Spirit, in solidarity with the poor? There is prayer that is about waiting on God, and listening—being willing to hear God's voice in those whom the world does not wish to hear, in "the pain of the landless," the "sigh of the oppressed" (p. 124). There is a prayer of longing for the "restlessness" of God to be born in us (p. 131)—restlessness for a kind of change of direction in the world that begins within us, but does not stop there.

There is the prayer of confession that recognizes in the power of the Spirit the seeds of hope, that there may be no need to focus "only on the past, repeating its violence, deepening its divisions" (p. 133).

The Spirit was promised as the one who would lead us into all truth. Aware of the power of the media, and of the competing and "dissonant voices" (p. 136) of ideologies that distort our perceptions, we pray for the capacity to discern the truth and that true gift of tongues, which is the courage to speak out for it. Only so can we "honor the Word eternal and speak to make a new world possible" (p. 134).

The Spirit is the source of all connectedness in love, and so we pray for what in our culture we deeply lack and that which communities of the poor so often demonstrate in abundance, namely a sense of connection with one another. Part of what makes it so hard for us to imagine the lives of the world's poorest, and to give support in a way that is not streaked with guilt, is our own experience of loneliness and lack of public warmth. So we pray also for ourselves, that the dry bones of our community may be knit together and breathed on by God. In this way we may know, from having received it, that sense of connection that the world's poor ask of us.

Above all, we find ourselves caught up in prayer that celebrates a God who is active, energetic, a transgressor of boundaries, the uncontainable source of all change. These prayers are full of *verbs* — describing both God's activity and our own, as we are drawn, with saints across the world and throughout history, into the dance of the Trinity. For the Spirit affirms what we most need to hear in our search for a just world, that "we are not alone" (p. 140). "Praise to the God who dances with us" (p. 132).

THE COMING OF THE SPIRIT

[1]

Lord, Holy Spirit,
you blow like the wind in a thousand paddocks.
Inside and outside the fences,
you blow where you wish to blow.

Lord, Holy Spirit,
you are the sun who shines on the little plant.
You warm it gently, you give it life,
you raise it up to become a tree with many leaves.

Lord, Holy Spirit,
you are the mother eagle with her young,
holding them in peace under your feathers.
On the highest mountain you have built your nest,
above the valley, above the storms of the world,
where no hunter ever comes.

Lord, Holy Spirit,
you are the bright cloud in whom we hide,
in whom we know already that the battle has been won.
You bring us to our Brother Jesus,
to rest our heads upon his shoulder.

Lord, Holy Spirit,
in the love of friends you are building a new house.
Heaven is with us when you are with us.
You are singing your song in the hearts of the poor.
Guide us, wound us, heal us. Bring us to God.

James K. Baxter, Aotearoa (New Zealand)
Your Will Be Done, Christian Conference of Asia Youth, 1984
Deuteronomy 32:10-12

[2]

In the depth of silence
no words are needed,
no language required.
In the depth of silence
I am called to listen.

Listen to the beating of your heart.
Listen to the blowing of the wind,
the movement of the Spirit.
Be silent, said the Lord,
and know that I am God.

And listen to the cry of the voiceless.
Listen to the groaning of the hungry.
Listen to the pain of the landless.
Listen to the sigh of the oppressed
and to the laughter of children.

For that is authentic communication;
listening to people
living with people
dying for people.

An Indonesian author, 1983
International Association for Mission Studies

[3]

O God, the source of our common life,
when we are dry and scattered,
when we are divided and alone,
we long for connection, we long for community.
Breath of God, breathe on us.

With those we live beside,
who are often strange to us,
whom we may be afraid to approach,
yet who have riches of friendship to share,
we long for connection, we long for community.
Breath of God, breathe on us.

With those we have only heard of,
who see with different eyes,
whose struggles we try to imagine,
whose fierce joy we wish we could grasp,
we long for connection, we long for community.
Breath of God, breathe on us.

With those we shall never know,
but whose lives are linked with ours,
whose shared ground we stand on,
and whose common air we breathe,
we long for connection, we long for community.
Breath of God, breathe on us.

When we are dry and scattered,
when we are divided and alone,
when we are cut off from the source of our life, open our
    graves, O God,
that all your people
may be free to breathe, strong to move,
and joyful to stand together
to celebrate your name. Amen.

Janet Morley, England
Christian Aid, 1990
Ezekiel 37:1-12

[4]

Spirit of God,
you are the breath of creation,
the wind of change that blows through our lives,
opening us up to new dreams and new hopes,
new life in Jesus Christ.

Forgive us our closed minds
    which barricade themselves against new ideas,
    preferring the past to what you might want to do
        through us tomorrow.

Forgive our closed eyes
    which fail to see the needs of your world,
    blind to opportunities of service and love.

Forgive our closed hands
    which clutch our gifts and our wealth
    for our own use alone.

Forgive us our closed hearts
    which limit our affections to ourselves
    and our own.

Spirit of new life,
forgive us and break down the prison walls of our
        selfishness,
that we might be open to your love
and open for the service of your world,
through Jesus Christ our Lord.
Amen.

Christopher Ellis, England, 1990
Isaiah 6:9-10

[5]

Come, Holy Spirit, and show us what is true.

In a world of great wealth
where many go hungry
and fortunes are won and lost
by trading in money,
   come, Holy Spirit, and show us what is true.

In a world of great knowledge
where many die in ignorance
and every piece of information
has a price in the market-place,
   come, Holy Spirit, and show us what is true.

In a world of easy communication,
where words leap between continents
and we expect to see a picture
to illustrate each item of the news,
   come, Holy Spirit, and show us what is true.

In a Church which speaks a thousand accents,
divided over doctrine, creed, and ministry,
more anxious for itself than for the Gospel,
   come, Holy Spirit, and show us what is true.

In a Church touched by the flame of Pentecost,
moved to generous sacrifice and costly love,
interpreting the will of God with new insight
   come, Holy Spirit, and show us what is true.

Stephen Orchard, England
All the Glorious Names,
United Reformed Church Prayer Handbook, 1989
John 16:12-15

[6]

Come Holy Spirit,
        enter our silences.
Come Holy Spirit,
        into the depths of our longing.
Come Holy Spirit,
        our friend and our lover.
Come Holy Spirit,
        unmask our pretending.
Come Holy Spirit,
        expose our lives.
Come Holy Spirit,
        sustain our weakness.
Come Holy Spirit,
        redeem our creation.

Enter our trusting,
enter our fearing,
enter our letting go,
enter our holding back.

Flood our barren spaces,
make fertile our deserts within.
Break us and heal us,
liberator of our desires.

Come Holy Spirit,
        embrace us and free us.
Amen.

Neill Thew, England, 1990

[7]

Exuberant Spirit of God,
bursting with the brightness of flame
into the coldness of our lives
to warm us with a passion for justice and beauty,
we praise you.

Exuberant Spirit of God,
sweeping us out of the dusty corners of our apathy
to breathe vitality into our struggles for change,
we praise you.

Exuberant Spirit of God,
speaking words that leap over barriers of mistrust
to convey messages of truth and new understanding,
we praise you.

Exuberant Spirit of God,
flame
    wind
        speech,
burn, breathe, speak in us;
fill your world with justice and with joy.

Jan Berry, England, 1990
Acts 2:1-21

[8]

Loving God,
Open our hearts
so that we may feel the breath and play of your Spirit.
Unclench our hands
so that we may reach out to one another
and touch and be healed.
Open our lips
that we may drink in the delight and wonder of life.
Unclog our ears
to hear your agony in our inhumanity.
Open our eyes
so that we may see Christ in friend and stranger.
Breathe your Spirit into us
and touch our lives with the life of Christ. Amen

Anonymous, Aotearoa (New Zealand)
Out of the Darkness: Paths to Inclusive Worship,
Australian Council of Churches, 1986
Isaiah 35:5

THE WORK OF THE SPIRIT

[9]

If you were busier, Lord,
you would not bother with us.
But you have time to listen.
**So we praise you
for having all things in proportion,
and a time in your silence for us to speak.**

If you were wiser, Lord,
you would not bother with us.
But you are foolish
and thus we are your choice.
**So, we praise you
that your kingdom is indeed upside down,
that your standards are not the world's standards,
that you have bent down to touch us.**

If you were content, Lord,
you would not bother with us.
But you are restless:
through anger, through excitement, and through love,
you will all things to change and be made new.
**So we praise you
that your restlessness has been born in us
as the pain of the world,
the cries of your people,
the urgency of your gospel,
and your Holy Spirit.
Upset our easiness
and require us to respond.**

Wild Goose Worship Group, *A Wee Worship Book*, 1989
Isaiah 43:18-19, 65:17-25; Hosea 11:4; Revelation 21:1-6

[10]

God, you invite us to dance in delight,
shaping and forming in figures of grace.
We move to the pulse of creation's music
and rejoice to be part of the making of earth.
**Praise in the making, the sharing, the moving;
praise to the God who dances with us.**

In the steps of Jesus we reach to our partners,
touching and holding and finding our strengths.
Together we move into patterns of freedom,
and rejoice to be part of the sharing of hope.
**Praise in the making, the sharing, the moving;
praise to the God who dances with us.**

We whirl and spin in the Spirit's rhythm,
embracing the world with our circles of joy.
Together we dance for salvation and justice,
and rejoice to be part of the moving of love.
**Praise in the making, the sharing, the moving;
praise to the God who dances with us.**

Amen.

Jan Berry, England, 1990

[11]

Wind of God, keep on blowing.
Sail over the barriers that we build
to divide ourselves from each other.
Pick up your seeds of freedom and truth wherever they
    flourish,
carry them across frontiers to be planted in other soil,
to begin fresh growth and new forms.

Blow from the South
to the ears of Northern peoples.
Blow away the blinders
which keep our eyes focused only on the past,
repeating its violence, deepening its divisions
and adding to its despair.
Reveal the new future you have in mind for us.

Fire of God, keep on burning,
smoulder in the hearts of people
where oppression keeps them in chains,
where unemployment and poverty devalue their humanity
and where hunger weakens the spirit.
Burn in them, like Moses' bush,
and do not let them be destroyed.

Tongue of God, keep on speaking
so that the peoples of earth
can speak your language to each other
and all can hear you in their own.

Speak peace where nations meet,
justice where ideas clash,
mercy where power reigns,
healing where minds and bodies hurt,
and love where churches seek your unity,
and wherever else Babel drowns out the sound of
    Pentecost.

Graham Cook, England
Say One for Me,
United Reformed Church Prayer Handbook, 1990
Genesis 11:1-9; Exodus 2:1-12; Acts 2:1-21

[12]

Let every word
be the fruit
of action and reflection.
Reflection alone
without action
or tending toward it
is mere theory,
adding its weight
when we are
overloaded
with it already.
Action alone
without reflection
is being busy
pointlessly.
Honor the Word eternal
and speak
to make
a new world possible.

Helder Camara, Brazil
The Desert Is Fertile, Orbis Books, 1974
Isaiah 55:8-11

[13]

Fount of all life, dancing in bliss,
Breaking down walls, making new space.

Burning up evil, creating afresh,
Calling your people, follow in faith.

Living with Jesus, power in his Name,
Healing the broken, restoring the lame.

134 PENTECOST

Casting out demons, raising the dead,
Calming life's storms, removing all dread.

Living to serve, confirmed from above,
Tested by fire, aflame with God's love.

Seeking the lost, sharing all pain,
Love at such cost, rising again.

Lighting our path, dancing ahead,
Leading through death, lifting to life.

United Theological College, Bangalore, India
"NOW," Methodist Church Overseas Division, 1988

[14]

For all the saints
    who went before us
    who have spoken to our hearts
    and touched us with your fire,
        we praise you, O God.

For all the saints
    who live beside us
    whose weaknesses and strengths
    are woven with our own,
        we praise you, O God.

For all the saints
    who live beyond us
    who challenge us
    to change the world with them,
        we praise you, O God.

Janet Morley, England
Christian Aid, 1989

[15]

Lord, forgive us, for we are fragmented persons.
We go many directions at once.
We seek opposite goals, we serve contradictory causes.
We mouth liberation, we live oppression.
We shout peace, we practice violence and anarchy.
We shout justice, we walk in injustice.
We preach love, we practice hate.
Through your compassion have mercy on us and make
     us whole.
Enable us to discern your voice among the dissonant
     voices.

What Does the Lord Require of Us?
National Council of Churches of the Philippines, 1989

[16]

My Lord is the source of Love; I, the river's course.
Let God's love flow through me. I will not obstruct it.
Irrigation ditches can water but a portion of the field;
the great Yangtze River can water a thousand acres.
Expand my heart, O Lord, that I may love yet more
     people.
The waters of love can cover vast tracts,
nothing will be lost to me.
The greater the outward flow, the greater the returning
     tide.
If I am not linked to Love's source, I will dry up.
If I dam the waters of Love, they will stagnate.
Can I compare my heart with the boundless seas?
But abandon not the measure of my heart, O Lord.
Let the waves of your love still billow there!

Wang Weifan, China
Lilies of the Field, trans. Janice and Philip Wickeri,
Foundation for Theological Studies in South East Asia, 1988

[17]

We believe in Jesus Christ,
our savior and liberator,
the expression of God's redeeming
and restoring love,
the mark of humanness,
source of courage, power, and love,
God of God,
light of light,
ground of our humanity.

We believe that God resides in slums,
lives in broken homes and hearts,
suffers our loneliness, rejection, and powerlessness.

But through death and resurrection
God gives life, pride, and dignity,
provides the content of our vision,
offers the context of our struggle,
promises liberation
to the oppressor and the oppressed,
hope to those in despair,
vision to the blind.

We believe in the activity of the Holy Spirit
who revives our decaying soul,
resurrects our defeated spirits,
renews our hope of wholeness
and reminds us of our responsibility
in ushering in God's new order here and now.

Yong Ting Jin, Hong Kong
In God's Image, 1986

[18]

Almighty God,
beginning and end;
giver of food and drink,
clothing and warmth,
love and hope:
life in all its goodness —
We praise and adore you.

Lord Jesus, carpenter's son;
lover of outcasts,
friend of the poor;
one of us yet one with God;
crucified and risen:
life in the midst of death —
We praise and adore you.

Holy Spirit, storm and breath of love;
bridge builder, eye-opener,
living power of Jesus;
waker of the oppressed,
God of the unexpected,
untameable energy of life —
We praise and adore you.

Holy Trinity, forever one,
whose nature is community;
source of all sharing,
in whom we love, and meet, and know our neighbor,
life in all its fullness, making all things new —
We praise and adore you.

Brian Wren, England
Christian Aid

[19]

We have heard about you,
God of all power.
You made the world out of kindness,
creating order out of confusion;
you made each one of us in your own image;
your fingerprint is on every soul.
So we praise you.
We praise and worship you.

We have heard about you,
Jesus Christ:
the carpenter who left his tools and trade;
the poor man who made others rich;
the healer who let himself be wounded;
the criminal on whom the soldiers spat
not knowing they were fouling the face of God;
the savior who died and rose again.
So we praise you.
We praise and worship you.

We have heard about you,
Holy Spirit.
You broke the bonds of every race and nation,
to let God speak in every tongue;
you made disciples drunk with grace;
you converted souls and emptied pockets;
you showed how love made all things new
and opened the doors to change and freedom.
So we praise you.
We praise and worship you.

Wild Goose Worship Group, *A Wee Worship Book,* 1989
Acts 2:1-21

[20]

We believe in a loving God,
whose Word sustains our lives
and the work of our hands in the universe.

God is life.

We believe in God's son among us,
who brought the seed of life's renewal.
He lived with the poor to show the meaning of love.

Jesus Christ is Lord.

We believe in the Spirit of Life,
who makes us one with God,
whose strength and energy renews our own.

The Spirit is love.

Camilo Torres, Colombia

[21]

We are not alone, we live in God's world.

We believe in God:
    who has created and is creating,
    who has come in Jesus,
    the Word made flesh,
    to reconcile and make new,
    who works in us and others
    by the Spirit.

We trust in God.

We are called to be the Church:
    to celebrate God's presence,

to love and serve others,
to seek justice and resist evil,
to proclaim Jesus, crucified and risen,
our judge and our hope.

In life, in death, in life beyond death,
   God is with us.

We are not alone.

Thanks be to God.

A New Creed, United Church of Canada
All Year Round, British Council of Churches, 1988

[22]

Look at your hands,
see the touch and the tenderness—
God's own for the world.

Look at your feet,
see the path and the direction—
God's own for the world.

Look at your heart,
see the fire and the love—
God's own for the world.

Look at the cross,
see God's Son and our Savior—
God's own for the world.

This is God's world
and we will serve God in it.

Wild Goose Worship Group, *A Wee Worship Book*, 1989

ORDINARY TIME:
TO FEED THE HUNGRY,
TO CARE FOR THE EARTH

Pentecost (for most Protestant faith traditions) and Ordinary Time (for the Roman Catholic tradition) comprise the greater part of the church year, and emphasis is placed on the life and work of the church. Collects and opening prayers call attention to many of the same themes: embracing God's will, seeking strength to follow God's call, showing love to one another, living in God's presence in justice, using wisely the blessings given to us by God, and sharing them with our brothers and sisters. The prayers that follow focus on these themes, with particular emphasis on providing for the needs of the poor and the hungry, and caring for the earth.

As we highlight concerns for the world's poor, including concern for those whose harvests have failed, or for those who for whatever reason do not enjoy the earth's fruits in security as we do, we realize our dependence on the earth and on the labor of many unseen hands.

But the more we explore some of the international connections on which we depend for the food we buy, the more we realize that the harvest that results cannot be celebrated in a simple or triumphalist way. Many of the connections are sinister, with increasingly oppressive consequences for poor peasants and poor countries, as they plunge further into debt, their crops exported to Northern countries at prices determined by others. The forest-stripping and mining methods of many transnational corporations whose products are household names frequently pollute the rivers, erode the soil, and destroy the flora and fauna of a region for ever.

There are those in the churches who find it objectionable to focus on such awareness, but Christian worship has never traditionally sought to offer thanksgiving that omits any mention of human betrayal. At the heart of the eucharist, we recount that it was "on the night that he was betrayed" that Jesus "took bread, gave thanks, and broke it." Food and drink are material symbols regularly included in our worship. They have a real material history, which can include the betrayal of justice, and it is right to offer that too. In this way, the gifts we present to be the body and blood of Christ are also "our witness against hunger, our cry against injustice" (p. 152).

Environmental "green" issues have become fashionable in the church as elsewhere. Realizing the dangers the earth faces from our greed and exploitation of its resources, many in our culture are seeking spiritualities that have taught a reverence for creation that the Christian West has effectively lost sight of. These have often resided in the wisdom of tribal groupings whose way of life is as threatened as the forests that have sustained them. We can learn from these faiths, but we can also re-learn to pray with those strands of our Christian heritage — the Franciscan and Celtic traditions — that proclaim our kinship and connection with the elements of the natural world. These affirm an incarnational faith that honors created matter and recognizes our bodies (which, as people who do not suffer hunger, we commonly forget) as the place of prayer:

Bless to me, O God,
  Each odor that goes to my nostrils;
Bless to me, O God,
  Each taste that goes to my lips. (p. 167)

It is too easy for those of us who do not actually work with the earth to sentimentalize nature in a way that farmers do not. But it is "ungrounded" and naive to pray as if the natural world were a place of primal innocence, as it is "ungrounded" and arrogant to pray assuming we have the right to dominate the earth without respect for its continued life. Rather, we need to pray knowing ourselves to be part of the created order that is longing and struggling for completeness and redemption (Rom. 8:18-25).

In this way, we shall not be tempted to separate "environment" and "justice" issues—our concern for the health of the land and the question of how justly or unjustly the land is shared so that all may live. As a human community, how we produce our harvest from the elements of the natural world represents a choice for either life or death. We need to confess that in our slavery to sin we have frequently chosen death: "We confess we have not shared the land; we have broken our bond with the earth and one another" (p. 157). Only when we have offered ourselves and our choices to be transformed by the God "who wore our clay in Christ" (p. 157) shall we learn to celebrate that harvest feast, where "Nobody will stay hungry" (p. 145).

To Feed the Hungry

[1]

Come on.
Let us celebrate the supper of the Lord.
Let us make a huge loaf of bread
and let us bring abundant wine
like at the wedding at Cana.

Let the women not forget the salt.
Let the men bring along the yeast.
Let many guests come,
the lame, the blind, the crippled, the poor.

Come quickly.
Let us follow the recipe of the Lord.
All of us, let us knead the dough together
with our hands.
Let us see with joy
how the bread grows.

Because today
we celebrate
the meeting with the Lord.
Today we renew our commitment
to the Kingdom.
Nobody will stay hungry.

Elsa Tamez, Mexico
Luke 14:12-24

[2]

Listen to the water
              air
          and earth:
                      creation's treasure store.
They're wounded for the want
of being listened to;
they cry
and too few hear;
they slowly die
and too few mourn.

And yet
through those who give attention,
who stretch both hands
to touch, embrace, and tend;
through those who marvel, reverence, and kneel
and cup the water,
feel the breath of heaven,
and hear the humming earth,
a healing comes
and there are seeds of hope:
there is tomorrow
germinating in today.
Listen to the stories
              dreams
          and thoughts
                      of those who have no voice.
They're wounded for the want
of being listened to;
they cry
and too few hear;
they slowly die
and too few mourn.

And yet
through these who give attention,
who stretch both hands
to touch, embrace, receive;
through these who labor, claim their dignity
and drink the cup of suffering,
breathe winds of change,
and earth their dreams in struggle,
healing comes and there are seeds of hope:
there is tomorrow
germinating in today.

Be still.
Be just—
sharing in their truth.
In finding them,
you find yourself.

Kate Compston, England, 1990

[3]

God, you heap your love upon us
    like a parent providing for a family's needs,
        embracing a child with tenderness.

Forgive us
    when, like spoiled children,
        we treat your generosity as our right,
        or hug it possessively to ourselves.

Give us enough trust to live secure in your love
    and to share it freely with others
in open-handed confidence
    that your grace will never run out. Amen.

Jan Berry, England, 1990

[4]

We share a common earth.
We stand among each other.
We share our planet,
we share birth, death, hunger, and love.

The sky opens above us and we receive space.
The earth stands beneath us and we receive ground.
The air becomes our breath and we are one wind.
The water becomes our blood and we are one sea.
Living things die for us.
And we die, returning to soil, sea, and air.

We are the people of pain and fear,
we are the people of anger and joy,
we are the people of compassion and grace.

In all of us is a longing
for a life that has not yet come,
for a world that is free and just,
a dream of hope for all people.

> Adapted from a liturgy, Australia
> "Celebration of the Unity of All Humankind,"
> *Let All the World*, ed. Wendy Robins, USPG, 1990

[5]

Leave this chanting and singing.
Whom do you worship in this lonely dark corner of the
    temple with all the doors shut?
Open your eyes and see that God is not in front of you.

God is there where the farmer is tilling the hard ground
and where the laborer is breaking stones.
God is with them in the sun and the rain

wearing a garment covered with dust.
Put off your holy cloak
and like God come down onto the dusty soil.

Deliverance? Where will you find deliverance?
Our Creator has joyfully taken on the bonds of creation;
God is bound with us for ever.

Come out of your meditations
and leave aside the flowers and the incense.
What harm is there if your clothes become tattered and
    stained?
Meet God and stand by God in toil
and in the sweat of your brow.

Rabindranath Tagore, India
2 Corinthians 8:9

[6]

All hands together
to change the world.
All hands together
to till the land.
All hands together
to pull up weeds.
All hands together
to share our joy.

Pastoral Team of Bambamarca, Peru
Vamos Caminando: A Peruvian Catechism, Orbis Books, 1985

[7]

Seeds we bring
Lord, to you, will you bless them, O Lord!

Gardens we bring
Lord, to you, will you bless them, O Lord!

Hoes we bring
Lord, to you, will you bless them, O Lord!

Knives we bring
Lord, to you, will you bless them, O Lord!

Hands we bring
Lord, to you, will you bless them, O Lord!

Ourselves we bring
Lord, to you, will you bless us, O Lord!

> Adapted from an East African hymn used at Seed
> Consecration Service
> *Morning Noon and Night*, ed. John Carden, CMS, 1976

[8]

O God, whose word is fruitless
when the mighty are not put down,
> the humble remain humiliated,
> the hungry are not filled,
> and the rich are;
make good your word,
and begin with us.
Open our hearts and unblock our ears
to hear the voices of the poor
and share their struggle;

and send us away empty with longing
for your promises to come true
in Jesus Christ.
Amen.

Janet Morley
Tell Out My Soul, Christian Aid, 1990
Luke 1:46-53

[9]

Brothers and sisters in creation, we covenant this day with
you and with all creation yet to be:
with every living creature and all that contains and
sustains you;
with all that is on earth and with the earth itself;
with all that lives in the waters and with the waters
themselves;
with all that flies in the skies and with the sky itself.

We establish this covenant, that all our powers will be
used to prevent your destruction.

We confess that it is our kind who put you at the risk of
death.

We ask for your trust and as a symbol of our intention we
mark our covenant with you by the rainbow.

This is the sign of the covenant between ourselves and
every living thing that is found on the earth.

Covenant Declaration at Winchester Harvest
Celebration, England
Lord of Creation, Worldwide Fund for Nature,
Yorkshire Television, 1987
Genesis 8:22, 9:8-17; Hosea 2:18-23

[10]

What do you bring to Christ's table?
We bring bread,
made by many people's work,
from an unjust world
where some have plenty
and most go hungry.

At this table all are fed,
and no one turned away.
Thanks be to God.

What do you bring to Christ's table?
We bring wine,
made by many people's work,
from an unjust world
where some have leisure
and most struggle to survive.

At this table all share the cup
of pain and celebration,
and no one is denied.
Thanks be to God.

These gifts shall be for us
the body and blood of Christ.
Our witness against hunger,
our cry against injustice,
and our hope for a world
where God is fully known
and every child is fed.
Thanks be to God.

Eucharistic prayer by Brian Wren and Betsy King, England
Let All the World, ed. Wendy Robins, USPG, 1990
1 Corinthians 11:17-29

To Care for the Earth

[11]

O Eternal Wisdom,
who laid the foundations of the earth,
and breathed life into every creature,
creating us in our variety
to cherish your world and seek your face:
we praise you and give you thanks
for your abundant love toward this earth,
violated with our injustice,
and polluted by our sin;
you took upon you our unprotected flesh,
and entered our struggle,
that you might deliver all creation
from its bondage to oppression and decay.

Therefore, with those whose voice is silenced,
with those who call for freedom,
those whose harvest celebration
sings through hardship and labor and love;
and crying with them for that new creation
when the morning stars shall sing together,
and all the children of God shout for joy,
we praise you, saying (or singing):

Holy, holy, holy,
all-creative God,
heaven and earth are full of your glory.
Hosanna in the highest.

Janet Morley, England
Till All Creation Sings, Christian Aid, 1989
Job 38

[12]

Lord,
isn't your creation wasteful?
Fruits never equal
the seedlings' abundance.
Springs scatter water.
The sun gives out
enormous light.
May your bounty teach me
greatness of heart.
May your magnificence
stop my being mean.
Seeing you a prodigal
and open-handed giver,
let me give unstintingly . . .
like God's own.

Helder Camara, Brazil
The Desert Is Fertile, Orbis Books, 1974
Psalm 104:27-30

[13]

O God, our creator,
whose good earth is entrusted
to our care and delight and tenderness, we pray:

For all who are in captivity to debt,
whose lives are cramped by fear
from which there is no turning
except through abundant harvest.

May those who sow in tears
reap with shouts of joy.

For all who depend on the earth
for their daily food and fuel
whose forests are destroyed
for the profits of a few.

May those who sow in tears
reap with shouts of joy.

For all who labor in poverty,
who are oppressed by unjust laws,
who are banned for speaking the truth,
who long for a harvest of justice.

May those who sow in tears
reap with shouts of joy.

For all who are in captivity
to greed and waste and boredom,
whose harvest joy is choked
with things they do not need.

May those who sow in tears
reap with shouts of joy.

Turn us again from our captivity,
and restore our vision,
that our mouth may be filled with laughter
and our tongue with singing.

Janet Morley, England
Till All Creation Sings, Christian Aid, 1989
Psalm 126

[14]

Long live this wounded planet
Long live the good milk of the air
Long live the spawning rivers and the nurturing oceans
Long live the juice of the grass
and all the determined greenery of the globe
Long live the surviving animals
Long live the earth, deeper than all our thinking.

We have done enough killing.

Long live the man
Long live the woman
Who use both courage and compassion
Long live their children.

Adrian Mitchell, England
Ride the Nightmare, Jonathan Cape, Ltd.

[15]

God, our creator,
you have made us one with this earth,
to tend it and to bring forth fruit;
may we so respect and cherish
all that has life from you,
that we may share in the labor of all creation
to give birth to your hidden glory,
through Jesus Christ.
Amen.

Janet Morley, England
All Desires Known, 1988
Genesis 2:7-9, 15-17

[16] LITANY OF THE FOUR ELEMENTS

Leader: Earth, air, fire, and water are traditionally
symbols of life. Our "slavery to sin" has meant
that these elements may equally carry and
contain death.

Life: I am life. I offer earth to share between the
daughters and sons of God—soil for bearing
plants to sustain the planet's life and yield bread
for all people.

(A bowl of earth may be presented.)

Death: I am death. I take earth away from the many
and give it to the few. I exploit and over-use it. I
waste its bread, while many starve.

Leader: O God, who wore our clay in Christ,
we confess we have not shared the land;
we have broken our bond with the earth and
one another.

All: **Forgive us: we have chosen death.
We long for healing: we choose your life.**

Life: I offer air to breathe;
for the endless energy of the wind,
for birds to fly and seeds to blow.
Air has no frontiers; we share the breath of life.

(Feathers and winged seeds may be presented, or an
open-armed gesture made as if to present the air around
the speaker.)

Death: I fill the air with poisonous fumes which all must breathe, and which claw away the threads of the universe.

Leader: O God, who breathed life into the world,
we confess that we have polluted the air;
we cannot sense the harmony of your creation.

All: **Forgive us: we have chosen death.**
We long for healing: we choose your life.

Life: I offer fire for light and warmth, for purification and power. Fire draws us together in fellowship, around a meal cooked and shared together.

(A candle may be presented.)

Death: I use fire for my own violent ends.
I burn the forests and choke the air.
I give the rich the earth's energy to waste.
I deny the poor their fuel to cook with.

Leader: O God, pillar of fire and pentecostal flame,
we confess our lack of inner fire
for your justice to be done,
your peace shared on earth.

All: **Forgive us: we have chosen death.**
We long for healing: we choose your life.

Life: I offer water to drink and cleanse;
to be the veins and arteries of the land;
I offer strong waves for energy,
and still lakes for calm of spirit.

(A bowl of water may be presented, or the congregation may be sprinkled with water.)

Death: I pollute water with waste from the mines and
factories, that it may kill the fish, be bitter to
drink, and carry disease.
I withdraw water from the land and make a
desert;
I extend the waters of the sea and drown cities.

Leader: O God, fountain of living waters,
we confess that we are cracked cisterns,
lacking stillness to listen to your word,
and energy to act on it.

All: **Forgive us: we have chosen death.
We long for healing: we choose your life.**

Leader: God of earth, air, fire, and water,
we surrender to you our old humanity.

All: Christ, we would rise with you:
we would be born anew.

Leader: **Christ has died: Christ is risen.
We are forgiven: we too may leave the grave.**

Kate Compston, England
Christian Aid, 1991
Romans 6:3-11

[17]

Listen now. Be still and hear.
For creation takes up its Maker's call. All creation draws
near to God, seeks refuge from the tightening grip of
winter, the winter our destruction has wrought; seeks light
and warmth to revive that which we have darkened and
chilled by our abuse of God's creation.

Listen to the voices of Creation.

Air: Lord, I the air come. Breath of life,
        wind that moves over the face of the deep.
        Bearing rain, I come.
        Now the breath of life blows death.
        As I pass over the land, the broken soil follows me;
        a billowing shroud of dust.
        When the rain falls, forests and lakes die.
        I come, my Lord.
        But what have your people made of me
        but a shadow, a dark acidic shadow,
        of my God-given glory.
        Breathe on your people, breath of God.

All: **Breathe on your people, breath of God.**

Water: We the Waters come, O Lord, flowing to meet
        you,
        as we have flowed through time,
        sustaining the life of all creation.
        We come, O Lord, from our rivers and lakes,
        our seas and oceans.
        We come, O Lord, with our dead upon our waves.
        Our living struggle against creeping filth
        and our mighty creatures flee
        before the fury of your people.
        Can we ever recapture the purity of your will

in the brightness of our waters?
Stir up your people, O Lord,
to let waters flow with life everlasting.

All: **Stir up your people, O Lord.**

Land: Mountain and valley, hill and plain,
        we the Land turn to you, our Lord,
        Ground of our ground.
        Upon us you set your world,
        from us you called forth life in many forms.
        In our richness you set the forests.
        On our fields you sowed the seed of life.
        Gone are our forests, worn is the earth.
        Silent in their graves lie the riches of your creation.
        Gouged out are our mountains,
        gone are the curves of our valley.
        We who would bear your creation seek re-creation.
        Plant in your people a love and respect for your
        Land.

All: **Plant in your people a love and respect for your
        land.**

Martin Palmer and Anne Nash
Advent and Ecology, World Wide Fund for Nature, 1988

[18]

Deep peace of the running wave to you;
deep peace of the flowing air to you;
deep peace of the quiet earth to you;
deep peace of the shining stars to you;
deep peace of the Son of Peace to you.

Celtic blessing
Celebrating Together, Corrymeela Press, 1987

[19]

May the blessing of light be on you,
   light without and light within.
May the blessed sunlight shine upon you
   and warm your heart
   till it glows like a great fire
   and strangers may warm themselves
   as well as friends.

And may the light shine out of the eyes of you,
   like a candle set in the window of a house,
   bidding the wanderer to come in
   out of the storm.

May the blessing of rain be on you;
   the soft sweet rain.
May it fall upon your spirit
   so that little flowers may spring up
   and shed their sweetness on the air.

And may the blessing of the great rains be on you,
   to beat upon your spirit and wash it fair and clean;
   and leave there many a shining pool
   where the blue of heaven shines,
   and sometimes a star.

May the blessing of the earth be on you,
   the great round earth;
may you ever have a kindly greeting for people
   as you're going along the roads.

And now may the Lord bless you,
   and bless you kindly. Amen.

            Irish blessing
            All Year Round, British Council of Churches, 1987

[20]

Grandfather,
look at our brokenness.
We know that in all creation
only the human family
has strayed away from the sacred way.
We know that we are the ones
who are divided,
and we are the ones
who must come back together
to walk in the sacred way.
Grandfather, sacred one,
teach us love, compassion and honor
that we may heal the earth
and heal each other.

From the Ojibway Nation of Canada
Our World, God's World, Bible Reading Fellowship, 1986

[21]

I believe, O Lord and God of the peoples,
that Thou art the creator of the high heavens,
that Thou art the creator of the skies above,
that Thou art the creator of the oceans below.

I believe, O Lord and God of the peoples,
that Thou art the One who created my soul and set its
    warp,
who created my body from dust and from ashes,
who gave to my body breath, and to my soul its
    possession.

The Celtic Vision, ed. Esther de Waal,
Darton, Longman & Todd, 1988

[22]

Most high, all-powerful, all good, Lord!
All praise is yours, all glory, all honor and blessing.
To you, alone, Most High, do they belong.
No mortal lips are worthy to pronounce your name.
All praise be yours, my Lord, through all that you have
        made,
    and first my Lord Brother Sun, who brings the day;
    and light you give to us through him.
How beautiful is he, how radiant in all his splendor!
    Of you, Most High, he bears the likeness.
All praise be yours, my Lord, through Sister Moon and
        Stars;
    in the heavens you have made them,
    bright and precious and fair.
All praise be yours, my Lord, through Brothers Wind and
        Air,
    and fair and stormy, all the weather's moods,
    by which you cherish all that you have made.
All praise be yours, my Lord, through Sister Water,
    so useful, lowly, precious and pure.
All praise be yours, my Lord, through Brother Fire,
    through whom you brighten up the night.
How beautiful he is, how cheerful, full of power and
        strength.
All praise be yours, my Lord, through Sister Earth, our
        mother,
    who feeds us in her sovereignty
    and produces various fruits with colored flowers and
        herbs.
All praise be yours, my Lord,
    through those who grant pardon for love of you;
    through those who endure sickness and trial.
Happy those who endure in peace,
    by you, Most High, they will be crowned.

All praise be yours, my Lord, through Sister Death,
   from whose embrace no mortal can escape.
Woe to those who die in mortal sin!
   Happy those she finds doing your will!
   The second death can do no harm to them.
Praise and bless my Lord, and give him thanks,
   and serve him with great humility.

St. Francis, *Canticle of Brother Sun*

[23]

Every part of this earth is sacred.
**Whatever befalls the earth befalls the children of the
      earth.**
The air is precious;
for all of us share the same breath.
This we know, the earth does not belong to us:
we belong to the earth.
This we know, all things are connected,
like the blood which unites one family.
Our God is the same God,
whose compassion is equal for all.
For we did not weave the web of life:
we are merely a strand in it.
Whatever we do to the web
we do to ourselves.

Adapted from a speech by Chief Seattle, 1854
Genesis 2:4-23

[24]

God of creation, the earth is yours
with all its beauty and goodness,
its rich and overflowing provision.

But we have claimed it for our own,
plundered its beauty for profit,
grabbed its resources for ourselves.

God of creation, forgive us.
May we no longer abuse your trust,
but care gently and with justice for your earth.
Amen.

Jan Berry, England
Psalm 24:1-2

[25]

Enjoy the earth gently
Enjoy the earth gently
For if the earth is spoiled It cannot be repaired
Enjoy the earth gently.

Yoruba poem, West Africa

[26]

May the road rise to meet you.
May the wind be always at your back.
May the sun shine warm upon your face.
May the rains fall softly upon your fields until we meet
    again.
May God hold you in the hollow of his hand.

Gaelic blessing

BLESSINGS

[1]

God to enfold me,
    God to surround me,
God in my speaking,
    God in my thinking.

God in my sleeping,
    God in my waking,
God in my watching,
    God in my hoping.

> *The Celtic Vision*,
> ed. Esther de Waal, Darton, Longman & Todd, 1988

[2]

Bless to me, O God,
    Each thing my eye sees;
Bless to me, O God,
    Each sound mine ear hears;
Bless to me, O God,
    Each odor that goes to my nostrils;
Bless to me, O God,
    Each taste that goes to my lips,
    Each note that goes to my song,
    Each ray that guides my way,
    Each thing that I pursue.

> *The Celtic Vision*,
> ed. Esther de Waal, Darton, Longman & Todd, 1988

[3]

As we prepare to leave
and embrace the challenges
of our lives and our world,
let us ask for God's blessing.

May God bless us with strength
to seek justice.   **Amen.**

May God bless us with wisdom
to care for our earth.   **Amen.**

May God bless us with love
to bring forth new life.   **Amen.**

In the name of God, the maker of the whole world,
of Jesus, our new covenant,
and of the Holy Spirit, who opens eyes and
hearts.   **Amen.**

Go in peace and be witnesses to hope.
Thanks be to God.

"Building a New World,"
Canadian Catholic Organization for Development
and Peace, 1991

Index of Prayer Types

In order to assist the use of these prayers in a variety of worship contexts, I have categorized them below according to broad type. Some will be found in more than one category, and it should be stressed that this is only a guide to use, and is not prescriptive. It is not necessary to explain what is meant by the traditional elements of the liturgy: adoration, thanksgiving, confession, intercession, and so forth. But it seems helpful to introduce some further categories in order to distinguish the material fully.

An *opening prayer* is one used to acknowledge the presence of God and to proclaim the themes of worship. It reflects a style of opening devotion common in the free church tradition.

Instead of the classic category of *petition* (prayers for ourselves), I have used the concept of *prayers of longing.* Among these are prayers that are primarily an *invocation* of God, either prayers describing waiting, or prayers crying out to God to come. There is also the *lament,* a form familiar to us from the psalms. It is a form of prayer as wrestling with God, and is forthright about pain, confusion, and anger, even anger with God — who has promised to answer the cry of the afflicted and yet often seems silent or absent.

There are several prayers of *challenge,* and these might be used as an invitation to admitting sin or to self-offering, or as a call to worship.

Words of forgiveness offer words that strengthen or reassure, and are appropriately used following the confession of sin and absolution.

Under *collects* we have included some prayers that follow the classic form of the collect, but also short prayers to use as alternatives or additions to the set collect, or at any time during worship when a short prayer is required.

Meditations are reflective prayers that open up thought and imagery in the contemporary world, in relation to a particular biblical passage or to one of the classic Christian doctrines of creation, incarnation, redemption, and so forth. They are suitable for use as opening prayers, as a comment upon the biblical passage when used as a reading in the service, or perhaps at the end of a sermon or homily.

Affirmations of faith include proclamations about God, about our hope, and about the stance we choose to take in the world and in relation to evil.

There are prayers that are *celebrations of the saints,* usable on traditional saints' days, but also to celebrate modern saints and martyrs of struggle—and indeed the communion of saints of which we are all a part.

Prayers around the *eucharist* include some that are suitable as preparation for communion or post-communion prayers, and some texts to be used as the great prayer of thanksgiving (in whole or part).

Prayers of self-offering are appropriately used with offertory prayers, as post-communion prayers, as prayers of commitment, or as a response to words of absolution following confession of sin.

1. Opening Prayers
2. Adoration
3. Thanksgiving
4. Prayers of Longing
   a. Invocation
   b. Lament
5. Prayers of Challenge
6. Confession of Sin
7. Words of Forgiveness
8. Collects
9. Meditations

10. Affirmations of Faith
    a. About Our God
    b. About Our Hope
    c. About Our Stance
11. Intercessions
12. Celebration of Saints
13. Prayers at the Eucharist
14. Prayers of Self-Offering
15. Final Prayers

1. Opening Prayers

Come humbly, Holy Child [ADVENT 1]
When I'm down and helpless [ADVENT 2]
You keep us waiting [ADVENT 3]
In the awesome name of God [ADVENT 7]
The desert will sing and rejoice [ADVENT 8]
Have you not heard about him [ADVENT 14]
The poor of the world are thirsty [ADVENT 17]
Open up the way for the people [ADVENT 18]
Come to the world [ADVENT 19]
All the broken hearts [ADVENT 24]
Helpless God as child and crucified [CHRISTMAS 3]
Choosing God [CHRISTMAS 4]
The Word, for our sake [CHRISTMAS 7]
This is the day [CHRISTMAS 11]
Through Jesus, our greatest treasure [CHRISTMAS 13]
We thought we knew where to find you [EPIPHANY 17]
Beckoning God [EPIPHANY 19]
God of gold [EPIPHANY 20]
What can we bring [EPIPHANY 22]
God, we praise you for your love in Christ [LENT 20]
Lord God, in Jesus, you came [HOLY THURSDAY 3]
The cross is the way of the lost [GOOD FRIDAY 17]
It is the Lord, in the dawning [EASTER 1]
God of power [EASTER 7]

In the depth of silence   [PENTECOST 2]
Exuberant Spirit of God   [PENTECOST 7]
If you were busier, Lord   [PENTECOST 9]
Almighty God, beginning and end   [PENTECOST 18]
We have heard about you   [PENTECOST 19]
Come on. Let us celebrate   [ORDINARY TIME 1]

2. Adoration

Blessed art thou   [CHRISTMAS 14]
God of power   [EASTER 7]
Alleluia. Speak, Jesus, Word of God   [EASTER 11]
Lord, Holy Spirit, you blow like the wind   [PENTECOST 1]
Exuberant Spirit of God   [PENTECOST 7]
Fount of all life   [PENTECOST 13]
Almighty God, beginning and end   [PENTECOST 18]
We have heard about you   [PENTECOST 19]
Lord, isn't your creation wasteful   [ORDINARY TIME 12]
Most high, all-powerful, all good, Lord   [ORDINARY TIME 22]

3. Thanksgiving

You keep us waiting   [ADVENT 3]
Today I look into my own heart   [ADVENT 10]
For the darkness of waiting   [ADVENT 12]
Holy Lord, some day   [ADVENT 20]
My soul magnifies the Lord   [ADVENT 22]
Thank you, scandalous God   [CHRISTMAS 12]
Risen Jesus   [EASTER 6]
O Lord our God   [EASTER 9]
If you were busier, Lord   [PENTECOST 9]
God, you invite us to dance   [PENTECOST 10]
For all the saints   [PENTECOST 14]

4. Prayers of Longing

a. Invocation and Search

Come humbly, Holy Child [ADVENT 1]
When I'm down and helpless [ADVENT 2]
You keep us waiting [ADVENT 3]
Who will set us free [ADVENT 5]
For the darkness of waiting [ADVENT 12]
O God: Enlarge my heart [ADVENT 13]
Come to the world [ADVENT 19]
Helpless God as child and crucified [CHRISTMAS 3]
Its outspread wings [EPIPHANY 18]
May it come soon [LENT 1]
Our Lord, who is in us [LENT 2]
The desert waits [LENT 14]
Come, Lord, do not smile [LENT 15]
My God, I need to have signs [LENT 17]
Lord God, in Jesus, you came [HOLY THURSDAY 3]
God, food of the poor [HOLY THURSDAY 5]
When the hour comes [EASTER 2]
Stay with us, Lord [EASTER 10]
In the face of the struggle [EASTER 19]
When the day comes [EASTER 20]
Lord, Holy Spirit, you blow like the wind [PENTECOST 1]
O God, the source of our common life [PENTECOST 3]
Come, Holy Spirit, and show us what is true
    [PENTECOST 5]
Come, Holy Spirit, enter our silences [PENTECOST 6]
Loving God, Open our hearts [PENTECOST 8]
Wind of God, keep on blowing [PENTECOST 11]
My Lord is the source of Love [PENTECOST 16]
Seeds we bring [ORDINARY TIME 7]

b. Lament

Who will set us free [ADVENT 5]
Holy Lord, some day [ADVENT 20]

O God of all youth   [ADVENT 21]
Wake up little baby God   [CHRISTMAS 8]
Its outspread wings   [EPIPHANY 18]
God of gold   [EPIPHANY 20]
You seduced me, Lord   [LENT 4]
Kumba Yah   [LENT 6]
God, freedom for the oppressed   [GOOD FRIDAY 7]
Bless your people, Lord   [GOOD FRIDAY 8]
Jesus, you have heard our tears   [GOOD FRIDAY 11]
With his hands   [GOOD FRIDAY 13]
In the pain, misfortune, oppression   [GOOD FRIDAY 14]
I believe, although everything hides you   [GOOD FRIDAY 16]
Merciful God   [GOOD FRIDAY 19]
Lord Jesus, by your cross   [HOLY SATURDAY 22]
Oh people, you shall not drown in your tears   [EASTER 15]
When we are all despairing   [EASTER 17]
O God, whose word is fruitless   [ORDINARY TIME 8]
O God, our creator   [ORDINARY TIME 13]
Listen now. Be still and hear   [ORDINARY TIME 17]

5. Prayers of Challenge

Come to this table   [CALL TO PRAYER 1]
Come to the living God   [CALL TO PRAYER 2]
When I come in the guise   [ADVENT 16]
Here I am   [CHRISTMAS 5]
Will you come and see the light   [CHRISTMAS 10]
Come, Lord, do not smile   [LENT 15]
Do not retreat into your private world   [LENT 11]
Holy God, holy and strange   [GOOD FRIDAY 9]
When we stand gazing upwards   [EASTER 5]
Let every word   [PENTECOST 12]
Look at your hands   [PENTECOST 22]
Leave this chanting and singing   [ORDINARY TIME 5]

6. Confession of Sin

Come humbly, Holy Child   [ADVENT 1]
If we have worshiped you   [ADVENT 6]
In the awesome name of God   [ADVENT 7]
Come to the world   [ADVENT 19]
From the cowardice   [CHRISTMAS 2]
Choosing God   [CHRISTMAS 4]
Lord, I am blind   [CHRISTMAS 9]
O God, who am I now   [EPIPHANY 16]
Our God and Lord   [LENT 8]
Come, Lord, do not smile   [LENT 15]
For our incapacity to feel   [LENT 18]
You asked for my hands   [LENT 23]
Lord, you placed me in the world   [LENT 24]
Holy God, holy and strange   [GOOD FRIDAY 9]
O Christ, in whose body was named   [GOOD FRIDAY 15]
Merciful God   [GOOD FRIDAY 19]
Above any government   [EASTER 8]
Stay with us, Lord   [EASTER 10]
Spirit of God   [PENTECOST 4]
Lord, forgive us   [PENTECOST 15]
God, you heap your love upon us   [ORDINARY TIME 3]
O God, whose word is fruitless   [ORDINARY TIME 8]
Litany of the four elements   [ORDINARY TIME 16]
Listen now. Be still and hear   [ORDINARY TIME 17]
Grandfather, look at our brokenness   [ORDINARY TIME 20]
God of creation   [ORDINARY TIME 24]

7. Words of Forgiveness

Have you not heard about him   [ADVENT 14]
All the broken hearts   [ADVENT 24]
This is the day   [CHRISTMAS 11]
Blessed are the poor   [LENT 19]
Soft the Master's love song   [EASTER 14]

Oh people, you shall not drown in your tears   [EASTER 15]
Deep peace of the running wave   [ORDINARY TIME 18]
May the road rise to meet you   [ORDINARY TIME 26]
God to enfold me   [BLESSINGS 1]

8. Collects and Short Prayers

Come God   [ADVENT 4]
God, our hope and our desire   [ADVENT 9]
God of the poor   [ADVENT 11]
From the cowardice   [CHRISTMAS 2]
God our midwife   [CHRISTMAS 6]
Wake up little baby God   [CHRISTMAS 8]
Through Jesus, our greatest treasure   [CHRISTMAS 13]
Blessed art thou   [CHRISTMAS 14]
What can we bring   [EPIPHANY 22]
Christ, our partner   [LENT 5]
O God, you claim me   [LENT 9]
God of vision   [LENT 16]
Spirit of truth   [LENT 21]
God, our promised land   [LENT 22]
God, food of the poor   [HOLY THURSDAY 5]
Hands like these   [GOOD FRIDAY 10]
Lord: Help us to see   [HOLY SATURDAY 23]
O God, whose word is fruitless   [ORDINARY TIME 8]
God, our creator   [ORDINARY TIME 15]

9. Meditations

Today I look into my own heart   [ADVENT 10]
My soul magnifies the Lord   [ADVENT 22]
Holy Child of Bethlehem   [CHRISTMAS 1]
Helpless God as child and crucified   [CHRISTMAS 3]
Choosing God   [CHRISTMAS 4]
Here I am   [CHRISTMAS 5]
The Word, for our sake   [CHRISTMAS 7]

Lord, I am blind   [CHRISTMAS 9]
Thank you, scandalous God   [CHRISTMAS 12]
Through Jesus, our greatest treasure   [CHRISTMAS 13]
Blessed art thou   [CHRISTMAS 14]
O God, who am I now   [EPIPHANY 16]
We thought we knew where to find you   [EPIPHANY 17]
Beckoning God   [EPIPHANY 19]
The cross points us to God   [HOLY SATURDAY 21]

10. Affirmations of Faith

a. About Our God

Firmly I believe, Lord   [EASTER 3]
We believe in God, creator of the earth   [EASTER 4]
God of power   [EASTER 7]
Alleluia. Speak, Jesus   [EASTER 11]
We believe in Jesus Christ   [PENTECOST 17]
Almighty God, beginning and end   [PENTECOST 18]
We have heard about you   [PENTECOST 19]
We believe in a loving God   [PENTECOST 20]
We are not alone   [PENTECOST 21]
I believe, O Lord and God   [ORDINARY TIME 21]

b. About Our Hope

The desert will sing and rejoice   [ADVENT 8]
We are wayfarers   [LENT 13]
God, our promised land   [LENT 22]
The cross is the way of the lost   [GOOD FRIDAY 17]
I believe that behind the mist   [EASTER 12]
Oh people, you shall not drown   [EASTER 15]
Life goes beyond death   [EASTER 16]
Goodness is stronger than evil   [EASTER 18]
When the day comes   [EASTER 20]
I am no longer afraid of death   [EASTER 22]

Come on. Let us celebrate [ORDINARY TIME 1]
Listen to the water [ORDINARY TIME 2]
All hands together [ORDINARY TIME 6]
Long live this wounded planet [ORDINARY TIME 14]

c. *About Our Stance*

We are called to proclaim the truth [ADVENT 23]
There is dignity here [EPIPHANY 15]
Let us name what is evil [LENT 12]
Blessed are the poor [LENT 19]
I believe, although everything hides you [GOOD FRIDAY 16]
We are the children of the sun [EASTER 13]
Say "no" to peace [EASTER 21]
We share a common earth [ORDINARY TIME 4]
Brothers and sisters in creation [ORDINARY TIME 9]
Every part of this earth is sacred [ORDINARY TIME 23]

11. Intercessions

When I'm down and helpless [ADVENT 2]
Open my eyes [ADVENT 15]
O God of all youth [ADVENT 21]
Holy Child of Bethlehem [CHRISTMAS 1]
Wake up little baby God [CHRISTMAS 8]
Its outspread wings [EPIPHANY 18]
May it come soon [LENT 1]
Kumba Yah [LENT 6]
A litany for the world we live in [LENT 7]
Blessed are the poor [LENT 19]
Lord God, in Jesus, you came [HOLY THURSDAY 3]
Bless your people [HOLY THURSDAY 8]
To you, O Lord [GOOD FRIDAY 18]
Above any government [EASTER 8]
In the depth of silence [PENTECOST 2]

Come, Holy Spirit, and show us what is true
    [PENTECOST 5]
Wind of God, keep on blowing [PENTECOST 11]
O God, our creator [ORDINARY TIME 13]

12. Celebration of Saints

Brother, let me be your servant [LENT 3]
We are wayfarers [LENT 13]
Blessed are the poor [LENT 19]
Nailed to a cross [HOLY SATURDAY 20]
We believe in God, creator of the earth [EASTER 4]
O Lord our God [EASTER 9]
We are the children of the sun [EASTER 13]
Life goes beyond death [EASTER 16]
For all the saints [PENTECOST 14]

13. Prayers at the Eucharist

Come to this table [CALL TO PRAYER 1]
Come to the living God [CALL TO PRAYER 2]
In the awesome name of God [ADVENT 7]
Thank you, scandalous God [CHRISTMAS 12]
My God, I need to have signs [LENT 17]
Lord Jesus Christ [HOLY THURSDAY 1]
We know that we come together [HOLY THURSDAY 2]
Eucharistic Prayer [HOLY THURSDAY 4]
God, food of the poor [HOLY THURSDAY 5]
Eucharistic Prayer [GOOD FRIDAY 6]
Come on. Let us celebrate [ORDINARY TIME 1]
What do you bring to Christ's table [ORDINARY TIME 10]
O Eternal Wisdom [ORDINARY TIME 11]

14. Prayers of Self-Offering

For the darkness of waiting [ADVENT 12]
O God: Enlarge my heart [ADVENT 13]

Open my eyes [ADVENT 15]
Lord, I am blind [CHRISTMAS 9]
My singing heart [EPIPHANY 21]
What can we bring [EPIPHANY 22]
Brother, let me be your servant [LENT 3]
Brother Christ [LENT 10]
We are wayfarers [LENT 13]
God, we praise you for your love in Christ [LENT 20]
You asked for my hands [LENT 23]
Lord, you placed me in the world [LENT 24]
Jesus invites us to a way of celebration [LENT 25]
When we are all despairing [EASTER 17]
Loving God, Open our hearts [PENTECOST 8]
God, you invite us to dance [PENTECOST 10]
My Lord is the source of Love [PENTECOST 16]
Look at your hands [PENTECOST 22]
Come on. Let us celebrate [ORDINARY TIME 1]
Seeds we bring [ORDINARY TIME 7]
Brothers and sisters in creation [ORDINARY TIME 9]
Lord, isn't your creation wasteful [ORDINARY TIME 12]

15. Final Prayers

Come God [ADVENT 4]
Open my eyes [ADVENT 15]
When the song of the angels is stilled [EPIPHANY 23]
O Lord Jesus [GOOD FRIDAY 12]
Alleluia. Speak, Jesus, Word of God [EASTER 11]
Let every word [PENTECOST 12]
All hands together [ORDINARY TIME 6]
Deep peace of the running wave [ORDINARY TIME 18]
May the blessing of light be on you [ORDINARY TIME 19]
Enjoy the earth gently [ORDINARY TIME 25]
May the road rise to meet you [ORDINARY TIME 26]
God to enfold me [BLESSINGS 1]
Bless to me, O God [BLESSINGS 2]
As we prepare to leave [BLESSINGS 3]